Seeds of Faith

To Glyn

with all good wishes
& love

Graham
Lent 2006

Seeds of Faith

Graham Neville

Shoving Leopard

Published by
Shoving Leopard
8 Edina Street (2f3)
Edinburgh,
EH2 5PN,
Scotland

http://www.shovingleopard.com

ISBN 1 905565 05 4 Paperback

Preface

We can take the parable of the sower as a parable about parables. What happens to the seed depends on the soil that receives it. So the parables of Jesus mean different things to different people, and bring about different results.

That is true of most forms of religious teaching. The word is spoken, with a more or less clear meaning in the mind of the speaker. In the listener's mind it may have another meaning and produce results unexpected by the speaker.

The thoughts offered in this little book can only be like seeds, growing differently, or just being barren, according to the mind of the reader. Their usefulness doesn't even depend on agreement with the intention in the mind of the writer. Meditation or discussion may be all the more valuable for the very fact of disagreement.

Perhaps the various pieces don't even agree with each other. The writer calls to mind the words of Walt Whitman: 'Do I contradict myself? Very well, I contradict myself! I contain multitudes.' Not multitudes perhaps, but certainly thoughts drawn from years apart. It would be surprising if they all agreed with each other. Remember Proverbs 26. 4 and 5: 'Answer not a fool according to his folly... Answer a fool according to his folly'. Or Matthew 12.30 and Mark 9.40: 'He that is not with me is against me... He that is not against us is for us.' Contrary things can both be true in different contexts.

Use these seeds as you wish. They might grow in meditation or discussion. They might lead on to prayer. Agree or disagree. The only wish of the writer is that every reader will be trying to fathom something of the mind of Christ. Rather as Paul wrote (Philippians 1.18) that he rejoiced that in any way Christ was proclaimed.

The texts at the head of each section show some point of departure or indicate some salient point in what follows. But they might be used, in a fuller form than the brief quotation, to lead out into broader fields of thought.

There is a section for the church's seasons and a general section, an

ABC of thoughts; but the arrangement is not important. So there is an index of key-words, and the reader can hop about, perhaps following up thoughts which originate elsewhere. At the end of the book is a collection of aphorisms - words without a context. For any one of them the reader may supply a context, and then nod assent or shake a disdainful head - or rewrite it nearer to the heart's desire.

A well-known seed firm carries on the front page of its catalogue the advice, 'Grow something new from seed'. That, too, is a parable.

May God give the increase.

Graham Neville
Worcester

Contents

Advent

Anxiety

Philippians 4.6 Have no anxiety

Whenever we are anxious, we are disobeying our Lord. Those are hard words, to be sure. There is not one of us who has not at some time or other been a prey to anxiety. Some people live their whole lives to an undertone of anxious thoughts, and yet they are not bad Christians. They live decent lives. They worship God. They help their neighbours. Perhaps they have every reason to be anxious. Perhaps the future really is clouded for them, or for someone they love. Is not their anxiety the very fruit of their love? If they had no loving sympathy for the difficulties and sufferings of others, they would not be anxious as they are.

If we must choose love with anxiety or coldness with freedom from care, how can a Christian hesitate to choose love, even though it brings anxiety with it?

But Paul boldly offers us the hope of freedom from anxiety, on two conditions. The first is that we bring everything into prayer - a continuous activity of supplication and thanksgiving. The second is that we keep ourselves aware of the nearness of God. The Lord is closer than our closest friends, at hand to help and heal, at hand to give us his peace which will keep our hearts and minds in Christ Jesus.

Choices

Luke 17.34 The one shall be taken and the other left.

The coming of the Son of Man means judgment, and judgment means separation. It will be like the flood, when Noah was saved and the rest perished through unbelief. It will be like the destruction of Sodom and Gomorrah, when Lot was saved and the rest perished because they would not repent. It separates those who look inseparable: two people in one bed, two women working at a mill. One shall be taken and the other left. It judges and divides. This is a matter of life and death. So said Jesus.

We see no sign of his coming. We confidently expect another ten, twenty, thirty, forty years of life. But we can't keep the judgment at arm's length. Why will one in the bed be taken and the other left? Not because of anything they were doing or thinking then, peacefully sleeping. Why will one at the mill be taken and the other left? Not because of anything they were thinking or doing at the mill, as their two arms pushed round the upper millstone by the same handle. The separation will happen because of the past, because of choices made long since, because of the kind of people we have already become. Today we make the choices which lead to separation.

Coming

Revelation 3.20   Behold I stand at the door and knock

The work of the ministry is to prepare men and women for a choice. The choice they must make is whether or not to say, Come Lord Jesus.

That does not mean, Come into the church, for he is in the church already, and not by our invitation. It does not mean, Come into the world, for he is in the world already, and not by our invitation. It means nothing else than this: Come into my life. For he cannot come there, except by our invitation.

There was a time when Christ came without invitation into the world. The shepherds on the hills were not thinking of the coming of Christ. The ordinary people of Bethlehem were not thinking about Christ and his coming. There was no invitation on the lips of King Herod, or the High Priest, or the leaders of the Pharisees. But Christ came in the stillness of a winter's night; and the only invitation was the willingness in the heart of Mary.

In the past Christ came, and in the future he will come, without invitation. But now he waits to be invited, and we must invite him every day. He comes with his demands; but he is also a paying guest. He pays with peace and power and the knowledge and love of his Father. If we know the true value of his gifts, we shall not count the cost of his coming.

Community

I Corinthians 16.22   Our Lord, come!

When we consider the infinitely patient way in which God fashioned the world and brought the human race into existence, it is impossible to believe that he will simply lose patience and say, Things are going badly; it's time to pack it all up. That cannot be the meaning of Advent. It isn't enough to think of the future in individual terms, as the trickling through of God's chosen people into another life somewhere else. It isn't enough to say that history isn't going anywhere in particular, like a cricket match in which the players are just playing out time.

So what else might Advent mean? The Bible begins in a garden and ends in a city; it begins with Eden and ends with the new Jerusalem. Those pictures tell us that what God is doing in history is one long act of creation - the creation of a kind of human society in which at last human beings can live together in peace because they are at peace with God. When that has been achieved, then Christ will have come in power and glory.

Whether that consummation belongs to time and to history; whether it will come by gradual change or sudden leaps; whether the coming of the Son of Man has other meanings - on such questions we may differ. But this much at least is part of the promised Advent

.

Face to face

Revelation 22.4 They shall see his face.

In John's description of the heavenly Jerusalem, the goal of all our journeying, he uses many images to convey his vision - the book of life, the tree of life, the river of life as clear as crystal. But no image can convey more than the five short words: They shall see his face.

That image means so much. To turn the face towards someone is to shew interest, be kindly disposed, and in the full meeting of eye with eye to show love. God has a face. He turns his face towards man. He cares for man, looking him in the eye with a look that is both searching and kind.

To see the face of God is to know him as he is, to look up with frankness and responding love, which is possible only to the innocent - or the forgiven. Because none of us is innocent, the face that looks up must bear the marks of contrition, of sorrow.

Until we reach the goal of our journey the face we see is the human face of Jesus Christ, or, as John calls him, the Lamb of God. That is not the face of God in all his majesty; but neither is it wholly different. Perhaps we can guess at this mystery by thinking of two images being brought into focus in a stereoscope, with a new dimension, the dimension of depth. We shall see the face of 'God and the Lamb'.

Incarnation

Hebrews 3.1 Wherefore, holy brethren

This holy God we worship did not simply create the world and then retire to a convenient vantage-point to watch it bring destruction on itself. Nor does he merely lay down the law of repentance for sinful man, and leave it at that. He became incarnate. He came down. He shouldered the burdens of the world. He submitted to its limitations, and yet made those limitations the language of his self-revelation. God's holiness is an otherness that has become ours, a strangenesss that has become akin.

If the holy God was incarnate, then to be 'holy brethren' means to take all that we have discovered and all that has been revealed to us and make it incarnate in our life, in our work, in our home, in all that we are and all that we do. Holiness begins with a secret life of dedication. It must end with the same outward movement of seeking which is to be seen in the holiness of God.

Judgment

Psalm 102.27 But you are the same

If God is always the same, we must be able to see the same pattern of God's dealings throughout the Bible. But perhaps to do so requires experience and practice.

Every now and again we hear about the rediscovery of a forgotten masterpiece of painting. In a junk shop or the storerooms of a museum an expert picks up an old painting in a battered frame. He blows the dust off it and glances at it - and then something makes him take another look. The magnifying glass comes out. The brushwork and pigments are examined with great care. He sees something in that neglected picture which has the imprint of a master's hand. He recognises a pattern.

In Old and New Testament, if we look carefully, we see a double pattern. Saving and judging. Graciousness and sternness. God creates out of love, and expels from Eden in judgment. God condemns the old world, and in love rescues Noah and his family. God destroys the cities of the plain, and blesses the seed of Abraham. Love and judgment are coupled together.

The same God comes in Jesus to save; yet his coming brings judgment. The pattern is repeated. God says, If you rebel, I will punish; but if you repent, I will restore.

Prophecy

Hebrews 1.1 God spoke of old to our fathers by the prophets

Some people say they feel very close to God when they are close to nature. In the beauty of the created world they feel the presence of God. Others say that in some ancient church or magnificent cathedral their hearts are lifted up and they are drawn to worship God.

But what nature and ancient buildings seldom, if ever, do is to bring home a direct command or promise or warning. They speak to our feelings more than to our wills. They speak of God, but do not tell us the word which God speaks.

Can the beauty of a tree's bare branches against a winter sky say to us, Do justly and love mercy and walk humbly with your God? Can an ancient cathedral say to us, Woe to him who builds his house by unrighteousness and his chambers by wrong? It is not things or buildings which give us God's commands, but men and women like the prophets of old. It would not be enough for the church to tell its members to go out into the wide open spaces on Sundays or visit ancient churches when they are empty. Both may be acts of worship. But to be faced with the commands and promises and warnings of God, you must hear the word spoken in scripture and preached in God's name.

Christmas

Childbirth

Luke 2.22 The days of her purification.

The idea of purification after childbirth offends us now. But that is largely based on a misunderstanding. The urgent imploring prayers of barren women in the Old Testament show that the birth of a child was to them supremely desirable. As the Psalmist said, Children and the fruit of the womb are an heritage and gift that cometh of the Lord.

But the Israelites were a people who believed in holiness, and by holiness they meant an almost tangible power, at work in the world, and specially at particular moments when human beings drew near to God: in sacrifice, in consecration - and in childbirth. That was the mysterious, awe-inspiring moment in which another of God's creatures began to breathe, to cry, to live in perilous independence, to set out on a journey through unforeseeable life. In giving birth the mother came within the sphere of holiness. It played about her as a divine aura, an influence, a force infecting her. Because she had entered the holy place, the sanctuary and shrine of procreation, she could not at once return to the realm of the secular, the mundane.

It is still true that childbirth is both natural and supernatural.

Force

Isaiah 42.3 A bruised reed he will not break

We are altogether too used to the methods of the world around us, where, in little things no less than in great, people try to get their way by some persuasion and, if that fails, by force. Often it seems the best we can do. But it is not the way of Almighty God.

When God chose to act decisively for man's salvation, he came, not with the visible might of armies, but in the helplessness of an infant and the defencelessnes of a man on a cross.

The coming of Christ is a continual reproach to us. Again and again we see no way to act but by a little persuasion and then by force. If it is the best we can do, God may pardon us in his mercy. But we must be clear in our minds that it is pardon we need. We can never be proud of our ways of power politics and of pressure and force in our dealings with one another. Our workaday actions come nearest to deserving praise - near and yet so far - as we try to take God's way and win and save the world by nothing but our humility and love and our readiness to suffer for those we are trying to help. Every act of force, even though we can see no other way to behave, is something for which we need to ask pardon.

Peace

John 14.27 My peace I give to you

What did Jesus mean by 'my peace'? We may be sure he did not mean a perpetual Sunday afternoon in summer. That is not what he offers.

In the Old Testament the basic meaning of peace is perfectness, completeness, fulfilment. People achieve what they call peace as they succeed in being what they think they are supposed to be. If their pattern of a human being is an elegant social creature, they find a sort of peace by being social and elegant. If they think they are meant to be materially comfortable, material things will give them a sort of peace. If they believe fulfilment comes from exercising power over others, they may find a sort of peace that way. But they do not find the peace of God.

God's peace means completeness after his original design. That is why Paul writes of Jesus Christ, 'He is our peace'. In Christ God's design for humanity is seen in its perfection. In his life he displays the pattern, and through his death he offers us the ability to be conformed to that pattern. The angels sang of God's peace at Bethlehem. The promise of Isaiah was fulfilled. 'Thou dost keep him in perfect peace whose mind is stayed on thee.'

New Year

Disappointment

Hebrews 1.12 You are the same, and your years will never end.

If you go out and stare up at the skies at night, you see the very same stars that your grandfather once saw, the same stars that Napoleon and Queen Elizabeth I and William the Conqueror once saw, the same stars that St Paul and Elijah and Moses and Abraham once saw, centuries ago. They circle and return, and they seem so permanent and unshakeable.

Yet the Psalmist, trying to express something he believed about God, could envisage the end of what seemed so everlasting, and say that even when that end came, God would be the same. 'They shall wax old like a garment; as a vesture thou shalt change them, and they shall be changed. But thou art the same, and thy years shall not fail.'

When the first bright flame of youthful hope dies to an ember, when we find that the world cannot easily be refashioned nearer to our heart's desire, when we learn by bitter experience that even firm friendships can falter, and that the things we have worked for most passionately bring disappointment in their achievement, nothing should make us confuse the eternal God with the transitory world he has made. He does not weary or grow old. He is the inexhaustible fountain of life, springing up for ever undiminished. And he is our God.

Epiphany

Miracles

John 2.5 His mother said to the servants, Do whatever he tells you.

A believing church is one which lives in daily expectation of miracles - the miracles of the spiritual life: changing hatred and ill-will to love and goodwill; the new life and love which come from forgiveness offered and received; selfishness turned into self-forgetfulness; a sinner repenting and beginning again on the road which leads to eternal life; an unbeliever convinced by the gospel; a man indifferent to the things of God making God his glory and the object of his worship. These are miracles, the work of the spirit of God.

If a believing church expects these miracles and they do not happen, what is wrong? If we want the seemingly impossible to happen, we must take to heart the words of Mary, 'Do whatever he tells you.'

Well, do we? Read the Sermon on the Mount and put it to the test. There and elsewhere in the gospel Jesus gives us practical things and inward things to do - practical things like praying together and inward things like forgiving to seventy times seven. So long as we hesitate and excuse ourselves, we shall never find out the reasons for his commands. Only our obedience can unlock his secrets and make miracles happen.

Obedience

Colossians 2.9 In him dwelleth all the fulness of the Godhead bodily

If I say to Christ, You are a good man, but your teaching is impractical, I cannot forgive till seventy times seven; then I am not worshipping. If I say to Christ, You are a good man, and I will obey you...unless I think you are mistaken; then I am not worshipping. If I say, You are very important, but I am important, too, and I want to lead my life as I please; then I am not worshipping. If I say, I will let you rule my religion, but not my business or my leisure; then I am not worshipping. If I say, I have done my best to obey you, and you must surely be pleased with me, still I am not worshipping.

The true worshipper stands before God with no rights, only duties; with no claims, only requests; with no self-awareness, only awareness of the one who is worshipful.

Paul says, In Christ dwells all the fulness of the Godhead bodily. Then let us adore him, Christ the Lord. And that will mean also, Let us obey him.

Lent

Paradox

Matthew 2.11 They fell down and worshipped him

The story of the Magi shows us a reversal of values. Wise men kneel before a child. Rich men humble themselves before the poor. Important men recognise their Lord in the offspring of an unimportant girl. And this reversal of values persists through the incarnate life. The unlearned is the world's greatest teacher, the glutton and the drunkard is the most disciplined of all, the enemy of sin is the friend of sinners, the demon-possessed works by God's own spirit, the helpless victim is the great High Priest, the crucified slave is the King of the Jews, and the defeated, deserted man is the Lord of life choired by angels, conquering and to conquer.

Paradox is piled upon paradox. It is part of the meaning of faith to be able to penetrate the veil of the commonplace and see, even now, the glory that lies concealed.

If we have learned to worship a crucified criminal and to call his cross the throne of glory, we shall not mistake the signposts along the pilgrim road. It will not be success but service that we follow as a beacon.

Eucharist

Exodus 20.10 The seventh day is a sabbath unto the Lord thy God.

The fourth of the Ten Commandments is about the rest of the Sabbath day. One way for the Christian to understand its deep meaning is to start from Jesus' saying: Man shall not live by bread alone, but by every word that proceeds out of the mouth of God.

Life, he says, consists of two parts: the part given up to bread (that is, to earning our daily bread, to work) and the part devoted to the word of God (that is, to receiving what we can't earn, the gracious word of God).

It is less important to make a difference between one day in the week and the other six, than to recognise that there are two elements, both necessary to the fulness of human life; the work of man and the word of God, what man can do to sustain his own life and what God alone can do to lift that life up to a higher level, the natural life of the body and the supernatural life of the spirit.

The principle of the Sabbath begins to be fulfilled in eucharistic worship, in which we receive God's manna, the living bread, the life of the Word from heaven. Time set aside for God means time to receive God's gift which we can never earn. What matters is not a particular attitude to a particular day, but the principle of finding time to receive the gifts of God.

God's children

Exodus 20.12 Honour your father and your mother.

One of the festivals of folk religion is Mothers' Day, or Mothering Sunday. And though no doubt Woolworths and Smiths would like it to have a fixed date it is still a movable feast, tied to the church calendar.

Great numbers of good-hearted people still go to the trouble to pick their bunches of flowers or buy their cards or presents for this day. And if we avoid sentimentality and prise ourselves free from the sexism which makes us think that the model of our relation with God must be that of a child with a father, surely we can see hidden away within those little sacrificial offerings something which corresponds with our offerings to God.

God brought us to birth. God taught us to be free. God waits and watches to see how we will use our freedom. As we slowly come to realise this, we present our little offerings to him. Their triviality does not matter, because they are symbolic. We cannot give back all we owe, because we owe to him our very being, our very freedom. God wills us to be, to continue to be, to continue to be free.

If we have grasped the meaning of the incarnation, we are not surprised to find this kind of correspondence between human relationships and our relation to God. We are on the look-out for glory hidden in the commonplace.

God's presence

Exodus 3.14 I am that I am

Self-examination and confession have their place in human life, to be sure. But sometimes it is better to try to forget about ourselves, and deliberately turn our attention to the truth of God. That truth is something we can neither create nor destroy. It would be just as true if we did not exist.

Listen, then, till you hear again the words which Moses heard at the burning bush. 'I am that I am.' Between one activity and another, he found himself in the presence and heard those words spoken. Between one activity and another we can try to hear his message. Does God not also say, 'You are, because I am'?

Perhaps we can find some help in the words of Jeremy Taylor:
'God is wholly in every place; included in no place; not bound with cords, except those of love; not divided into parts, nor changeable into several shapes; filling heaven and earth with his present power and with his never absent nature. So that we may imagine God to be as the air and the sea, and we all inclosed in his circle, wrapped up in the lap of his infinite nature; or as infants in the wombs of their pregnant mothers: and we can no more be removed from the presence of God than from our own being.'

Hope

I John 3.3 Everyone who has this hope before him purifies himself, as Christ is pure.

The natural man, without a religious faith, looking at his fellow human beings and himself, says that the one certain thing about the future is that we shall die. The one certainty is a dead certainty.

The person with faith, while not denying the reality of bodily death, adds another certainty about the future. The Christian says that, though many things remain uncertain, he or she will be made like the Lord Jesus Christ, reflecting the image of the one whose spirit is already at work within. God has no lower destiny in store for us.

This is the Christian hope. To be like Christ. To be endowed with his courage, his kindness, his determination, his self-forgetful love. That is as certain as death - more certain, in fact, since death will be destroyed, but this hope never.

But we are easily distracted from this hope, like watchers of the skies whose eyes are drawn away from a distant star by the flashing of a comet. It seems more exciting to look forward to fame or wealth or comfort, even a little fame. a little wealth, a little comfort. Have we lost sight of the greatest hope? John gives us a touchstone, a criterion. Are we 'purifying ourselves' - letting the dross be burnt away seven times in the fire?

Law

Matthew 5.22 But I say to you.

We are used to the idea that Jesus gave new meaning to the laws of Moses. He turned attention away from the acts of transgression to the motives of the heart - to hatred rather than murder, to lust rather than adultery.

Must that not mean that he was less concerned with the suffering caused by the action than with the sin committed? There is nothing sinful in suffering, or how could the perfect Son of God suffer? Suffering does not automatically separate from God; sin does.

If we are to accept the standards which Jesus set for us, we must read newspaper reports in a fresh way. When we read of a violent crime, our first reaction will be of sympathy with the victim. What about the harm done to the soul of the criminal? We need to feel in our hearts pity for the guilty as well as sympathy for the innocent.

That is not easy. We do not shudder at sin as much as we shudder at suffering. To shrink from suffering is natural and instinctive. To shrink from sin is supernatural.

In his revision of the law, Jesus showed that the real harm in the breaking the law is not just the threat to the stability of society so much as the threat to the soul of the sinner.

Mercy

Malachi 3.6 I the Lord do not change

There is a story in Genesis 18, which tells how God revealed to Abraham the coming destruction of the wicked city of Sodom, and how Abraham asked God to be merciful to it. He began by asking that it might be spared if there were fifty righteous men in it, and gradually reduced the number, till in the end God said he would not destroy it for the sake of just ten righteous men. It seems that Abraham beat down God in a kind of Dutch auction, and made God change his mind.

But perhaps that is only how it seemed to Abraham. We know how, when we look out from a railway train, hedges by the line side seem to swing past at a great speed, things in the middle distance not quite so fast, and distant objects only at a sedate pace. From another point of view the hedges and trees are stationary and only the traveller is moving.

So with the Genesis story. It seemed to Abraham that God was changing. In fact only Abraham changed, as he learnt that God was merciful.

In prayer we turn our thoughts to God. If we pray for something we want, we hold that up in the light of God's presence. Then we learn what God's will is. He doesn't change. Only we do.

Penitence

Isaiah 61.3 The garment of praise for the spirit of heaviness.

The Book of Common Prayer, some say, was written when life was painful and short. So all that the Reformers could see in the cross was how painful and short our sin made God's incarnate life. They over-stressed human sin and their masochism doesn't suit us today. So at the Lord's table let us eat, drink and be merry, for we shall never die. Sweep away this penitence, and shout aloud our praise.

Others say, This shallow age has no time for penitence because it has surrendered to self-regarding hedonism, even in religion. After Hiroshima and Nagasaki, after Belsen and Buchenwald, in an age of terrorism and massacre and man-made starvation, what we need is not less but more penitence.

We can only say, Lord, have mercy upon us. Must we choose? Are we to come before God with a kind of pious jollity, so glad for all that God has done that there is no room for self-concern, not even for the self-concern of the penitent? Or are we to kneel before God, hushed and shamed by human sin and its cost to the world God came to save?

Somehow we must do both, but in such a way that our praise will have a quality that no mere jollity can give, and our penitence will be flecked with thanksgiving, and sport a sheen unsuitable to mere mourning weeds.

Perfection

Colossians 3.14 Above all these, put on charity which is the bond of perfectness.

If you have on the table in front of you some separate pearls, each one has its own beauty as it lies there by itself. But if they are carefully graded according to size and then strung into a necklace, the result is something more than the sum total of the beauties of each particular pearl. The thread which holds them together, invisible though it is, produces an effect which the isolated pearls never could have achieved.

That suggests how charity, or love, is the bond of perfectness. It holds together the other virtues, and so creates an effect which the separate virtues by themselves never could have achieved.

Someone may be modest, truthful, honest, self-controlled, reliable - all virtuous characteristics - and yet lacking the very thing which binds together those virtues. Where everything is held together by the bond, or thread, of love, there is a quite distinct type of character. And this kind of love is not a general sentiment of goodwill, like the passing mood of amiability after a good Christmas dinner. In truth that has, in spite of its name, nothing to do with the will. Christian love is above all things an act of the will, often bent across the current of the affections and the mood of the moment.

Poverty

Matthew 5.3 Blessed are the poor in spirit.

Nowadays a 'poor' person is someone who hasn't been competitive enough and has lost out in the scramble for more money. But when Jesus spoke about the poor the word meant the godly poor or the suffering righteous. So in Matthew's gospel the beatitude concerns the poor in spirit - the spiritual poor.

If we ask what spiritual poverty means, there is a good answer in an old commentator who wrote, A poor man is he who cannot say, This is mine. In spiritual poverty, we recognise that all things come from God. We hold them only as a trust. The blessing of Christ is on those who achieve detachment from material possessions. That is equally difficult for the wealthy, whose aim has been to pile them up, and for those who are afraid of losing what little they have. It can only be achieved by valuing other things more highly than possessions.

One of the signs of this attitude which is emphasized in the New Testament is that of hospitality. It would be an incomplete Christian life which was never hospitable. But, of course, the principle of sharing privileges and pleasures can find expression in many other ways. It is hard to see how there can be a true spirit of poverty within if some such conscious sharing is not visible as the outward fruit.

Pride

I Peter 5.5 God opposes the proud, but gives grace to the humble.

One of the stock characters we meet in the gospels is the proud Pharisee, the one who doesn't know what is meant by self-criticism. Looking at him, we are presented with a choice between humility and pride. Humility depends on the practice of self-criticism. But it doesn't mean depreciating humanity in general or ourselves in particular. It doesn't involve regarding ourselves as vile creatures, but rather distinguishing what is our true place in creation and our true glory.

Our place in creation is as members of the kingdom of God, the realm of God which is everywhere. Our glory consists in doing God's will in a way unique to human beings. There must be other ways in which other creatures of God fulfil his purpose in creation. Our way is a conscious way - discovering God's will for us and freely making it our own.

To do this we may have to look to Gethsemane for a pattern - obedience at all costs may mean a sombre glory. We may have to admit that often that place and that glory have been bartered for lesser things, for a mess of pottage. But it is no true humility to settle for less than God's will for us. We must humbly ask for his grace to reach our exalted destiny.

Reconciliation

Matthew 5.24 Be reconciled to your brother.

Conflict is part of the world in which men and women have free wills. We have to accept that fact, and then release into situations of conflict the power of transforming love.

That rules out any question of demanding 'unconditional surrender'. It is hardly even possible that all the right is on one side and all the wrong on the other. Instead we are called to follow the way of Christ, which is the way of reconciliation. He has broken down the partition walls which separated Jew and Gentile, bond and free, male and female, identifying himself with all.

Must there not be other walls to break down, in order that peace may grow? God beseeches us in Jesus Christ, be reconciled. To whom? Well, what about the powerful? Tax collectors and sinners surely didn't think of themselves as in need of any one's pity. They had money and power. And somewhere in every conflict there is money and power. The way of Jesus was to stand alongside them.

Reconcilers need to stand firmly for the right, and firmly alongside those who are in the wrong. For that, we have to begin by becoming aware of what is wrong within ourselves. Only then can we begin the work of reconciliation.

Saul

Galatians 1.13 The Jews' religion.

The essence of the faith of Saul the Jew (who is also called Paul) was this: that there is but one God; that this one God, who created the world and mankind as the crown of creation, requires not merely the performance of certain ritual actions or the offering of material sacrifices, but far more importantly the keeping of a moral law; and that the moral law had been revealed in detail to the people of Israel in the scriptures, and especially in the books of the Torah.

We can't understand Saul's spiritual pilgrimage unless we see that that was his starting point. And of course these beliefs are contrary to what most people take for granted today. The world was not created by God, but by accident. There isn't one God so much as a kind of general spirit of good will or a life-force working equally in all things. Moral laws are not the requirements of a just God, but rather rules conveniently invented by society and put down to God's account to make people take them seriously. There is nothing specially inspired about the Old Testament, least of all the first five books.

If we share these beliefs, we shall find it hard to understand Paul. Or, for that matter, Jesus.

Talents

Matthew 11.5 The blind receive their sight.

There are different ways in which we may be aware of God - as moral demand, as perfect love, as the creator of all beauty, or as maker, sustainer, and redeemer of all things. These ways correspond to different aspects of the inner life of a human being: conscience, affections, sense of beauty, and intellect.

In self-examination we usually examine our lives only for moral lapses. But we should also be on the look-out for blindness in other faculties of the inner life.

If God demands that we use to the utmost each of the talents which he has given, is it right to think we shall be less blamed for failing to develop our appreciation of poetry or music, or failing to use our minds in his service, than for failing to keep our conscience alive?

We need to ask ourselves whether we are blind in any of the faculties of the inner man. Can I regard murder or adultery merely as the occasion of an intriguing news report? Can I accept the love and care of my family without a warm response? Can I look unmoved at the splendour and terror of the created world? Is my intellect blind to the questions which God, through his world, is posing today? From all blindness of heart, good Lord, deliver us.

Passiontide

Authority

John 13.4 Jesus girded himself with a towel

At the Last Supper Jesus is the host, presiding by right over the people of God, symbolically present in the twelve who were to sit on thrones judging the tribes of Israel. This is regal, lordly. But then with complete self-possession and unhurried calm, but with acute poignancy, he presents to them another role, the role of the suffering servant. He performs the menial act of the feet-washing. He is the servant, not only of God, but of men. He is the humblest of the humble.

The picture of Jesus kneeling to wash his disciples' feet challenges us. Don't we want a King Messiah - someone to run the world against its will for its own good? Don't we want a bit of prestige and respect for what we believe in - our church, our creed, our standards? It is hard to understand the figure and form of the servant.

Well, what about Jesus? Didn't he know how men ought to live? Hadn't he received a special commission from the Father? Wouldn't he be justified in taking the short cut of authoritarianism to set the world to rights?

But in the wilderness he had rejected those thoughts. Instead of a diadem he chose a towel - the proper prelude to the cross. Both were the prerogatives of a slave.

Betrayal

Mark 14.19 Is it I?

In more than one of the Psalms we read about betrayal. 'Even mine own familiar friend, whom I trusted, who did also eat of my bread, hath laid great wait for me.' Bitter thoughts about betrayal are easy to understand. For if friendship is the greatest of natural blessings, its betrayal is the most unnatural of crimes.

That crime is at the centre of the Passion story; it is the wood of which the cross is made.

Go back in imagination to the upper room where Jesus sat with his disciples. The act of sharing food was a sacred thing, cementing trust and friendship. Soon Jesus would take a towel and wash the feet of his friends. We can sense the warmth of friendship that was like an enfolding atmosphere, the very air they breathed. And then Jesus said, One of you will betray me, and each one of them wondered, Is it I?

We too have our times of warm devotion. Then perhaps we remember those words of Jesus, and are afraid of our own weakness, or cowardice, or blindness. But here is the wonder of the thing. To ask, Is it I? is the beginning of grace. He says, I have overcome the world. Together we will conquer, you and I.

Habits

Luke 22.19 He took bread, gave thanks, and broke it.

Is it too shocking to say that Jesus gave thanks from force of habit? Many times he had taken meals with his friends and presided at their common table by natural right. He must often have said the words of the traditional graces, and now in the very act of saying those traditional words his mind would be riveted on their meaning. Then, despite the blackness of the future, despite the shadow of death which fell across the scene, despite his misgivings about the courage of his disciples, he would bless God from his heart - for his goodness in all the works of creation, for his goodness to the people of Israel, for his plan of redeeming his people through the death of his servant, for giving the bread and the wine and for giving the body and blood with which the perfect sacrifice could be offered.

What is it that brings out the best in anyone in the moment of stress but good habits? The soldier calls them discipline, the doctor professional standards. Others speak of the sense of honour or the force of training. By whatever name, it is the same steady purposeful practice of good actions in the past which enables the right choice in the moment of crisis. We need good habits.

Humility

Philippians 2.8-9 He humbled himself...wherefore God has highly exalted him.

How hard it is to be humble! We can listen to words commending humility and even watch with the eye of our imagination the Son of God humbling himself to the death of the Cross, and go out from church or rise from reading our Bible and at once become self-assertive, unwilling to admit a fault, unwilling to ask pardon, unwilling to make amends, for fear we should let other people think themselves superior. Can we prove how wrong they are to think so by doing the very same thing ourselves?

It is only through humility than anyone can enter upon exaltation. There was no other way for Jesus. There is no other way for us.

If we stand on one side of a valley and look across to the higher hill on the other side, we know we cannot reach that height without first going down and crossing the stream. However brightly we imagine the joys of union with Christ and reunion with those who have gone before us, we can never reach that height of happiness without first going through the humiliation of death and all that it means of becoming weak and helpless and dependent on others, and finally letting go altogether. There must be humility first, even humiliation, and only afterwards glory.

Sacrifice

John 6.51 The bread which I shall give for the life of the world is my flesh.

The gospels make it clear that the feeding of the multitude in the wilderness and the last supper and the church's eucharist are connected and explain each other. All three are equally expressions of a law of life, perceived by Jesus, embodied by him in certain deliberate actions, and handed on to his disciples in the eucharist he invented.

That law is the law of sacrifice. It begins with little things - a boy's picnic buns. It begins with worldly things - bread and fish and money and all the things that money buys. It ends with the sacrifice of life itself.

That scholarly cynic A.E.Housman was never further from the truth than when he wrote:

Give crowns and pounds and guineas
But not your hearts away.

Jesus gave his heart away. He gave his life away - and found it again in the resurrection. He gives his life away in every eucharist, and finds it again in the new life of men and women who feed upon his sacrifical gifts. And still in a hundred thousand lives the law of sacrifice is repeated.

The Cross

Psalm 55.5 Horror overwhelms me.

How should we respond to horror stories? There is a horror story at the heart of Christianity - the story of the crucifixion. Perhaps we can learn something from the way the early church seems to have responded to it.

If Mark is the earliest gospel and John probably the latest, we see in the words from the cross that they moved from the idea of defeat and disaster (a God-forsaken Messiah on a criminal's cross) to triumph and achievement (God's most wonderful work carried through to completion). On the way, in Luke, the stress is on reconciliation, the supreme man in the throes of agony bridging the chasms of sadism and crime, drawing all humanity to himself and so into the very heart of God. Committing his own spirit to the Father, he brought with him the sinful, from whom he had never let himself be separated in his ministry.

Perhaps this movement meets our psychological needs. When horrible things happen, we need to cry out, God, why have you deserted us? There are outrageous things and we need to be outraged. But we need to move on, to find some flickering flame of heroism or love or forgiveness. Then a dayspring rises to disperse the horror of great darkness and once again we can commit our spirits into God's hands.

Easter

Death

Galatians 2.20 The life which I now live in the flesh,
I live by faith in the Son of God.

Boswell to Dr Johnson: Suppose a man who has led a good life for seven years commits an act of wickedness and instantly dies, will his former good life have any effect in his favour?

Dr Johnson: Sir, depend upon it, he will have the reward of his seven years' good life. God will not take a catch of him.

'Thou most worthy Judge eternal, suffer us not, at our last hour, for any pains of death, to fall from thee' (From the traditional Burial Service of the Book of Common Prayer).

The trouble with the (unscriptural) words of the old Burial Service is that they imply that God might well 'take a catch of us'. But both passages show a lively sense of the fragility of earthly life. Because it is fragile, it has to be lived in faith, and then it can have that quality which is indicated by calling it 'eternal'. The imperishable hills which have seen countless generations come and go are inextricably tied into this world. Fragile, perishable man, knowing himself mortal and soon to pass away is summoned by that very fact to live the life of faith, believing not only that he will rise again, but also that he is here and now the kind of being who can rise. He is resurrection-shaped.

Doubt

Matthew 28.17 When they saw him, they worshipped; but some doubted

The powers of death had been conquered. Christ had risen in triumph. Here surely was no room for doubting. But Matthew says, They worshipped him; but some doubted. Evidently God would not force them to believe.

Fearing doubt, people search for infallibility. Sometimes they think they have found it in the bible or the church or the inner light. But if the appearances of the risen Christ were not of such a sort as to compel belief, have we any reason to think that God, who required man's faith to come out and meet his revelation at that point, would set in the world something which would in future compel assent by its very infallibility?

There cannot be an act of faith which makes faith thereafter unnecessary. For faith is trust in a person. It would be absurd to think that two people who fell in love would not need to go on loving. It is absurd to think that one act of trust need not be followed by a life of trusting.

Matthew goes on to say that Jesus came and spoke to the disciples. That is the way doubts are resolved: through persons, not things. God does not give us a book or an institution or a brain-washing inner light. We have to trust a saviour.

Eternal Life

Hebrews 6.5 The powers of the age to come.

The Eucharist is a sacred meal which constitutes an intimate bond between those who share it. But what is the nature of the community which it creates? One answer in the New Testament is that the participants 'have tasted the powers of the world to come'. They have a first instalment of the life to come, they have seen the trailer of the big film, they have been given a free sample. Heaven is already here. Or, we might say, the coming of Christ has disrupted time and space.

Usually we think of our life on earth as followed consecutively by the life of another world. Or else we may think of the life of that other world as existing simultaneously but on a higher plane.

These models or pictures in the imagination have been disrupted by the advent of God incarnate. The present age is dragged forward into the age to come; or this lower world is heaved up into the higher. We have life eternal here and now.

The community, then, is four-dimensional. It has a side open to eternity. In fact, most of its members are on that side. The visible community is only a fraction of the whole. We of the church visible have our own particular business; no doubt they of the unseen church have theirs. Together we laud and magnify God's glorious name.

Joy

John 16.22 No one will take your joy from you.

To hold an Easter faith means to believe in the joy, not just as much as, but more than, the suffering; to believe that the joy is the thing that will remain, a joy that no one can take away.

The question is, whether this seems a reasonable faith, or not. That may depend on what we pay attention to in the world about us. For we are not human microphones registering equally all that comes within range. We select what we hear and see by acts of attention.

The Easter faith will seem reasonable if we attend to all those things which tell us of joy coming out of sorrow, from every normal human birth to the large-scale deliverances of whole peoples and nations from oppression or disease. The Easter faith is a declaration that these are the significant events for our understanding of the world. Their multitudinous evidence draws attention more and more to the one supremely important event for the Christian believer, the triumph of Jesus through the suffering of the cross. All the little moments when joy overcomes sorrow are mirrors which reflect the bright light of the resurrection. In its light we can go on believing that somehow, within this universe or beyond it, all sorrows will be overcome by joy. The Lord is risen.

Leisure

I Corinthians 15.58 Work for the Lord always.

Is it the goal of human life to be as idle as possible? We hope rationally for an early and adequate pension or fantastically for a jackpot in the lottery. Both hopes are of release from labour with all one's faculties intact. Is that the hope of the resurrection?

The lightening of the burden of necessary labour when strength declines is surely not contrary to the gospel. Much of the work by which people earn their living is irksome and exhausting and unfit for the old and infirm. But what do we want to retire for? For mere idleness? For an old age of trivialities? For the scrap-heap of human society?

There will always be 'work for the Lord', within a resurrection pattern. That pattern is repeated time and time again. The infant dies, that the child may be born. The child dies, that the youngster may be born. The youngster dies that the adult may be born. The adult dies, that the elder may be born. Each stage, with its characteristic excellence and its characteristic 'work', is raised up transformed in the next. At last the believer faces the final transformation, not into idleness and boredom, but into fuller life.

Life

Acts 2.24 It was not possible for him to be held by death.

Someone once said to me, 'I suppose I shouldn't say this' (that's a danger signal) 'but I have found the church quite unhelpful'. I was put out, and said edgily, 'Have you really tried it all? It's quite large, you know.' Immediately the barriers were up, and there was no trust between us, and life lost its quality, and I was thoroughly miserable.

It showed me that what made life worth living - the kind of life that deserved not to perish - was when there was communication between people - sympathy, understanding, the desire to help, readiness to be helped. We are divided from God and from each other by barriers of self-concern.

Real life is in Jesus Christ, who was always open to God and man, always letting God's life flow into him and through him to others. He was caught up in God's life and the life of all his fellow human beings. And so, of course, he could not be held by death. If we have already given our lives away in trust to those we meet daily, we need not fear death.

Trust

I John 3.2 It does not yet appear what we shall be.

Before the march of science the barriers fall. The barrier of time crumbles, as the living image and voice of the dead are brought back by the recording of sound and sight. The barrier of space crumbles as it becomes possible to circle the earth in a few brief hours and the spaces of the heavens begin to give up their secrets.

But one barrier at least baffles our assault - the barrier of death. Before that we fall back defeated. Even those who have claimed to make contact with the dead fob us off with vague generalities about a place of harmony and peace.

Christians believe that one traveller has gone the way of all flesh and returned to those who had known him before. Yet even Jesus in the miraculous forty days does not seem to have spoken of that strange journey. So St John says, It does not yet appear what we shall be.

Our ignorance of a life beyond death is a special instance of our ignorance about the future. However much we think we know about tomorrow, there is much about it that we cannot know. How shall I stand up to its unexpected challenges? I can only go forward in trust. So at last, facing death, I have a simple choice. I must trust God, or trust nothing.

Victory

John 10.15 I lay down my life

The paradox of the Easter victory is this - that both sides in the struggle want the same thing, the crucifixion of Jesus. It is no less willed by Jesus himself than by the priests and Pharisees and the common people. Both sides, too, claim the victory, when that death is accomplished. When Jesus on the cross cries out, It is finished, those words expressing the assurance of victory might just as well have been heard from the lips of Caiaphas. He too believed that he had won a victory for God and for Israel.

The victory of Easter Sunday is utterly unlike any victory in war. The method of Christ is to refuse to make use of the enemy's weapons. He is not even concerned to frustrate the enemy's will and prevent him doing what he set out to do. The warfare of Christ does not end with the surrender of the enemy. And Christ's victory is unlike victory in warfare in this as well: that no new enemies can ever win. Whatever they do, they cannot defeat God, whose love rises triumphant, not over their defeat, but over their victory

Ascension

Heaven

II Corinthians 12.2 I know a man in Christ..caught up to the third heaven.

Heaven is a problem - or so people often think. Even if we rule out some of the more mundane meanings the word has been given ('dancing cheek to cheek'?), we are left with two problems: its location and its life.

The second of those is the one that deserves greater attention. So decide what you mean by the life of heaven. When your mind is reasonably clear about that you can, if you like, try to locate it in the current picture of the universe, or out of it. But don't worry if you wake up tomorrow to find that the chart of the universe you were using has been demolished by cosmologists

The life of heaven is ineffable, beyond our telling. We begin to live it here and now. Already there are experiences which cannot be told. They may begin in childhood, while the innate sense of wonder is untarnished. They may come back in first love, in best love, in parenthood, or mediated by nature or beauty - so secret that human lips may not repeat them.

When the poet's lips are dumb
Then has inspiration come.
When the poet's lips are dry
He has found eternity.

Already in this everyday world the real seekers discern the life of heaven. The earth is one of its outposts.

Love

John 14.3 That where I am, there you may also be.

The Christian faith is full of improbabilities. It does seem so improbable - at Christmas time that God in his incarnation should show such care for mankind, when we care so little for each other - at Easter that someone should rise from the dead, when decline and death are the normal fate of all things living - at Whitsun that we should be enabled to have God dwelling within our hearts, which are so wilful and so hospitable to envy, hatred and malice - at the Ascension that our humanity should be exalted to heavenly places, when we find in ourselves a law of sin which stops us living even up to our own standards.

The Christian message is hard to accept because we have not grasped the mystery of God's being, as perfect love controlling perfect power. If we could believe in perfect love, we should not think it improbable that God should humble himself for our sake. If we could believe in perfect power, we should not think it improbable that God should raise Jesus from the dead. If we could believe in perfect love and power, we should not think it improbable that God should indwell and master us for love's sake, or that he should one day exalt us to heaven as he exalted his first-begotten son.

Responsibility

John 16.7 It is for your good that I am leaving you.

It must be better to be without the visible presence of Christ - better, not easier or more comforting. We are not meant to be for ever children, running to a heavenly nanny to have our questions answered and our fears and doubts resolved. We are meant to shoulder ever greater responsibilities.

That surely is obvious from the course of history. Once upon a time a chieftain might have been responsible for a few hundred of his clan. His failure could mean no more than the death or enslavement of a handful of followers. Today a few politicians have in their hands the bodies and souls of the whole human race. Unless history is quite out of hand, God must intend his human creation to carry more and more responsibility.

That is part of the meaning of the Ascension. It denies us a readily available authority for the solution of all problems. But we are not simply responsible for ourselves. We have to take responsibility for each other. This is another part of the meaning of the Ascension. It is as though Christ purposes to direct attention away from himself in his human body, in order that we may be led to look for him 'in face of friend and stranger'.

Pentecost

Family

Ephesians 4.3 The unity of the spirit.

In the gospels the family is sometimes presented as an enemy of Jesus, something that may claw back a potential disciple. One possible reason, said Jesus, for turning down God's invitation to the banquet of the kingdom is the pull of the family. Jesus himself had to break loose from family ties to do God's will.

Yet he spoke of God as father, and that must mean that at its best the love of parents for their children mirrors the loving care of God. Nevertheless like all good things the family may come between the disciple and the Lord.

Fanatical groups of all ages have claimed to possess the whole truth and the right to isolate converts from all social contacts. How can we distinguish between the claims of Jesus and the claims of dangerous or evil fanatics?

Perhaps the answer is in keeping together two simple words which are very important in the New Testament: 'one' and 'free'. A true family or community is marked by unity, yet in such a way that each member is free - free to be himself or herself to the full, with gifts and graces unlike those of any other member. Communities and families must be built on unity and freedom. That is in fact what we mean by the work of the Holy Spirit.

Pairs

Mark 6.7 He began to send them out two by two.

Philip and James. Simon and Jude. All other apostles are commemorated separately; these four come in pairs. Yet they were all sent out in pairs to proclaim the kingdom. Elsewhere too Jesus seems to throw emphasis on doing things together. If two agree on a petition, God will accept it. Where two or three are gathered, there is Christ. The missionaries in Acts go out in pairs: Paul and Barnabas, Paul and Silas, Barnabas and Mark.

Two people can spur each other on to greater efforts or check each other's faults. But there is more to it than that. We can use various images. The electric lamp that needs a negative and a positive pole. Gilbert's words intriguing, Sullivan's music memorable; together magical in their appeal. A duet quite different from two solos. A married couple quite different from two single people. In the meeting of two, for prayer, for study, for work or witness, there is new power, new light, new life.

No doubt there are deep experiences which can't be shared. A poet once wrote, of the invitation to confession:

Now are our prayers divided, now
Must you go lonelily, and I.
For penitence shall disallow
Communion and propinquity.

And yet we can release new power and light and life simply by drawing near to another.

Together

John 14.26 The Comforter will teach you all things.

Eleven men, eleven lives, and those lives leading by diverse routes to one place at one time: a first-floor room in Jerusalem at Passover. None would have been there except for the twelfth man at table with them. Eleven men and a leader, after Judas had gone out into the night. That was where the promise of the spirit was made.

We have got out of the way of thinking it is important to be 'with one accord in one place'. The telephone and radio and television have broken down the dividing barriers of space. We can so easily communicate across hundreds of miles. So we talk about 'being present in spirit'. Instead of regarding that sort of presence as second-rate, we kid ourselves that it is just as good.

God made us with bodies, and it is entirely through our bodies that we express the thoughts and needs and desires of the spirit. We use words, gestures, expressions of our faces. To enjoy the unity of the spirit we have to prod our lazy bodies to go to an agreed place of meeting. Only then, in the togetherness which is both of the body and the spirit, can we claim the fulfilment of Jesus' promise that the Father would send the Comforter to teach the disciples the truth.

Creation and Harvest

Dependence

Romans 14.7 We do not live to ourselves, and we do not die to ourselves

If we watch a combine harvester crawl across a ripe field we are watching a kind of portable factory, consuming great quantities of energy in the performance of dozens of inter-related tasks. Behind that complicated machinery we should envisage legions of workers responsible for its design and assembly and maintenence. The field now seems a lonely place where once there would have been a crowd of reapers and binders and children chasing rabbits and women bringing out bread and cheese and bacon and beer. But the apparent isolation of the worker in the field is an illusion. He depends far more on a host of strangers than his great-grand-father ever did. 'We do not live to ourselves, and we do not die to ourselves'

We need each other. We depend upon each other. That was one of the central convictions of Jesus that made him burst the bonds of nationalism and give his life for the many. God has bound us together in a common humanity. He has made of one blood all nations. The truth about us, which we constantly try to run away from, is that our true happiness is to be found in sharing with others what others have made available to us - which is to say, all that we possess.

Disasters

Romans 8.20 The creation was subjected to vanity.

'All ye works of the Lord, bless ye the Lord: praise him and magnify him for ever.' Quite apart from mankind, the natural world reflects the glory of God, in its beauty, its intricacy, its complexity, its grandeur, and its mystery. Paul was no nature mystic, yet he could say that God's invisible attributes are visible in the things he has made.

Yet the world contains not only beauty and majesty, but disease and disaster and death. The noxious germ survives and multiplies; floods and earthquakes repeatedly destroy. The biblical writers said this was no part of the original design. Creation had been subjected to a curse, to frustration of its true purpose.

We may try to express their meaning by saying that the world need not have been created as we now see it. It was made like that because of the kind of creature God knew human beings would become. It is shocking because it was meant to shock. It would challenge humanity to ask questions about its own destiny. Even through suffering and bewilderment men and women might be drawn back to God. For, mysteriously enough, God was there even in the suffering. He was there on the cross he had made.

Nature

Luke 15.31 All that I have is yours.

What are these things that are ours because God is our Father? First, the whole wide world of nature. We look out on the world and know that we can trace in it the Father's hand. In the new life and hope of spring, in the growth and abundance of summer, in the ripeness of autumn, and in the clear sharp bracing air of winter. To the Christian the world is no strange alien thing. From the beauty of the stars to the hidden beauty of the crystals of frost, invisible except under the microscope. This is our Father's world, and it is ours by inheritance.

The natural world is the first part of the All that God has given to his children. The other part is the very All of which the natural world is an expression. God's other gift is his own company. God came down in the cool of the evening to walk with man. Set beside those words some others: In the evening he cometh with the twelve. One evening God walked with Adam in the garden. One evening God incarnate came to the upper room for the last supper. Where two or three are gathered in his name, he is here still.

God says, All that I have is yours: the world I made and my presence in the world - a great gift and a greater gift.

Praise

Hebrews 1.3 Upholding the universe by his word of power.

We cannot suppose that God has nothing else to do but look after us. We cannot think that he created the whole of nature, the whole sky full of whirling stars, just for our sakes. If we let our minds wander through this great and terrible universe we shall see it as full of immeasureable spaces empty of all save God. Even in this little world of ours there are great tracts bare of human habitation. These thoughts force us into humility. 'What is man, that thou art mindful of him, or the son of man that thou visitest him?'

Humility is the beginning of something better than thanksgiving: praise. So long as we use the words 'Thank God' in a conventional way, just for escaping evils, we are kidding ourselves that we can get on all right without God in between calamities, as though God's chief work is to rescue us when we fall. We need a vision of how God upholds this great universe all the time, and ourselves as a little part of it - providing, sustaining, restraining. Then thanksgiving, which is inclined to be self-centred, is turned into praise.

Prayer

Matthew 6.10 Thy will be done.

Prayer has changed. When people used to pray for the crops, they were praying for a co-operative enterprise in which God gave the increase, through the natural order of growth. But the balance of responsibility is very different in modern industry. No doubt every process relies upon dependable regularities. Water always boils at the same temperature. Metals melt each at its own particular heat, which can be known in advance. But manufacture isn't like leaving a crop to grow. Every stage depends upon human decision and human action. It's no use praying and hoping it will turn out all right.

So our prayers have changed. We think less of asking God to do what we can't, and more of trying to know his will in order that we may, not without his guidance, act upon what we discover he wants us to do. So prayer is not making a shopping list, but bringing our wills into line with God's will.

Prayer is the real bent and direction and desire of our lives. The prayer which God hears is the prayer of our lives and not of our lips. If my prayers say, I want to be holy, but my life says, I want to be rich, God knows which prayer we hope will be answered first.

Remembrance

Remembrance

Ecclesiasticus 44.9 There are others who are unremembered.

Who should we remember? Imagine the feeling in any church if it was proposed to remove all monuments which did not commemorate someone who had been either poor, meek, pure, a mourner, a peacemaker, or persecuted. But why? Our Lord came to overturn the standards of judgment by which unredeemed mankind decided who was and who was not worthy of remembrance. Why else do we venerate that symbol of degradation, the cross?

Jew and Gentile alike reckoned they knew who was worth remembering: the national heroes, the great lawgivers, the mighty fighters, the figure-heads of religion and the arts. Such men do live on in their works. But are they the ones Christians should remember? The words of Jesus the son of Sirach are familiar, 'Let us now praise famous men'; but the writer did better when he said that it is working people who maintain the fabric of the world, and 'in their handywork is their prayer'. (And even if that isn't quite what the writer meant, it's a deeply perceptive thought.) Their lives are symbolized by many enduring memorials, from the ziggurats of Sumeria and the pyramids of Egypt to the canals and railways and roads that both cut and link our landscape. God does not forget them. We should say, 'Let us now praise ordinary men – and ordinary women.'

War

II Corinthians 5.18   The ministry of reconciliation.

War breeds horror, and war breeds heroism. The best is inextricably mixed with the worst. The reason why we call war evil is not, as a younger generation is tempted to assert, because it prevents us enjoying ourselves. That kind of argument trivializes the issue. It cannot be that the universe has travailed through millennia to produce a creature whose highest aim is to stay alive so that it can eat and drink and be merry. But if the choice is between a warring world with its horror and its heroism and a condition of universal self-indulgence with the human race lost in the frantic search for pleasure, can we be sure we know the right choice to make?

The Christian case against war is not that it prevents pleasure or even that nothing good happens in war. It is rather that so long as it lasts war nullifies all efforts at reconciliation. Once it has broken out, there is no good way which an individual can pursue. The choice is between the impotence of pacifism and the guilt of war. Yet neither of these is as bad as the real sell-out, the life of mere self-indulgence which can offer no resistance to the power of evil. Nothing worth the name of peace can come from the quest for pleasure.

Anthology

A human person

Psalm 95.6 O come, let us worship.

A human person is both like an animal and unlike. Our whole outlook upon life depends on how we define that unlikeness. We might define it from an evolutionary stand-point as the development of certain abilities or faculties, such as the ability to make and use tools. Then it would follow that the true life of a human being consisted in the exploitation of those abilities. We should be most truly ourselves when most advanced in technology, and the goal of human effort would be to gain the greatest possible control of our environment.

The biblical writers assume that the essential difference which sets us apart from other animals lies not in an ability but in a relationship. A human person stands in a conscious relation with God. That relation means sin and judgment, redemption and salvation. No animal can sin or be judged; no animal can be redeemed and brought to salvation.

By contrast, the process of sin and salvation is a long detour by which man is brought back to where he ought to be, what he was created for - a relationship of worship. The goal of human striving is represented more truly by the poor and humble and perhaps ignorant on their knees than by the most brilliant intellect which worships nothing but its own success.

Ambitions

Philippians 2.13 God is at work in you.

If, greatly daring, you had gone to King Herod Agrippa I and told him that in 1900 years' time hardly anyone would know anything or care anything about him, he might have been sensible enough not to be surprised. But if you had told him that millions of people would every year recall and give thanks for that man James bar-Zebedee whom he had put to death, he would no doubt have been frankly incredulous.

That is just one example of the shocking reversals of human judgment which are brought about in the counsels of God. It is God's good pleasure to upset human values and human judgments.

Can we apply that to ourselves? What are we really aiming to achieve in our lives? Our ambitions may be modest. We want, perhaps, a house that it is a pleasure to live in, the good opinion of our friends and neighbours, comfort without luxury and good repute without fame. We have our living to earn and we naturally want a certain amount of success in life. Yet at the heart of the matter, these things are not of great importance. In the eyes of God they are slight things. What we do or achieve is of transitory significance, little more than a flash in the pan. What really matters is what God achieves in us.

Anxiety

Philippians 4.6 Have no anxiety.

Whenever we are anxious, we are disobeying our Lord. Those are hard words, to be sure. There is not one of us who has not at some time or other been a prey to anxiety. Some people live their whole lives to an undertone of anxious thoughts, and yet they are not bad Christians. They live decent lives. They worship God. They help their neighbours. Perhaps they have every reason to be anxious. Perhaps the future really is clouded for them, or for someone they love. Is not their anxiety the very fruit of their love? If they had no loving sympathy for the difficulties and sufferings of others, they would not be anxious as they are.

If we must choose love with anxiety or coldness with freedom from care, how can a Christian hesitate to choose love, even though it brings anxiety with it?

But Paul boldly offers us the hope of freedom from anxiety, on two conditions. The first is that we bring everything into prayer - a continuous activity of supplication and thanksgiving. The second is that we keep ourselves aware of the nearness of God. The Lord is closer than our closest friends, at hand to help and heal, at hand to give us his peace which will keep our hearts and minds in Christ Jesus.

Armour

Ephesians 6.11   Put on the whole armour of God.

A popular writer of the last century, Henry Drummond, once tried to make a parable of the 'evolutionary mistake' of the hermit-crab in retreating into a borrowed shell and so losing the use of its legs. Is the armour of God that kind of shell? Will the Christian who regards his faith as a defensive armour find some of his spiritual faculties withering away?

I may say, I have the truth and have nothing to learn from the world; I am righteous and can sit in judgment on worldly people; I have faith which puts me right with God, never mind what happens to the world; I possess salvation, though the world goes to destruction; I have listened to the word of God, though it is nonsense to the world - then the armour is indeed like the hermit-crab's shell.

But I might say, I have been given the truth to share with others; I have been given the righteousness that comes by faith, and so I can go out helping others to find the same righteousness; I have been given salvation, a wholeness and health of spirit which sets me free to love my neighbour; I have been given God's word of forgiveness that speaks to the needs of all - then the armour of God is no carapace of self-righteousness, but a metaphor for the confidence with which I can face the world.

Christ

Matthew 25.37 Lord, when was it that we saw you?

'I turn to Christ.' Yes, but where is he? He is not on the cross. He is not in the tomb. He is not on the mountain top. To turn to Christ is not to turn to the past, to the far away and long ago Christ of Galilee and Judea.

As in the resurrection stories, he comes and goes, unhindered by walls or locked doors. When we repent of our sins and renounce evil, we do not turn for sanctuary to a church from which the world has been shut out. We face the challenge of the parable in which the King calls to his right hand those who fed him, gave him drink, welcomed him, clothed him, visited him, in the person of any who were in need.

The Christ to whom we turn is indeed wherever two or three are gathered in his name. He is indeed wherever the broken bread is received as his body and the wine as his blood. But he is no less present in the needs and sufferings of the world.

If we turn to him, we shall discover that his magnetic attraction makes us point in different directions at different times - now to the fellowship of all who like us have said, I turn to Christ, now to the hidden Christ, present in the humanity of our neighbours. Our solitary, even lonely, decision to turn to Christ throws us into the arms of others.

Civilization

Jeremiah 35.16 The sons of Jonadab the son of Rechab have kept the command which their father gave them.

The Rechabites mentioned in the Book of Jeremiah regarded all the apparatus of so-called civilized life with the greatest suspicion. They lived in tents, rejected agriculture and refused to drink wine. For two hundred and fifty years they had maintained the principles of the man whose name they bore. Jeremiah disagreed with them - and blessed them. Perhaps they were wrong; but they were gloriously, splendidly wrong. Their error was like a halo to their heads.

The ordinary Israelite accepted what the Rechabites rejected. The development of civilized society could not be reversed by the eccentricities of a few tent-dwelling teetotallers. The ordinary Israelite was right, but how miserably, how un-heroically right. He accepted the trend of history, which was, in a general way, the working out of God's purpose. But he did not try to understand what that purpose might be. God spoke, and he did not listen.

We, too, are not without our puritans and protestors. Perhaps they are wrong. Perhaps we are right to accept all that technology gives us. But if so, we are ingloriously, un-heroically right, unless we listen when God calls us to use it all to build his kingdom.

Consecration

I Corinthians 4.7 What have you that you did not receive?

Changes in liturgical practice have familiarized most worshippers with the offertory procession at the eucharist.

The Reformers of the sixteenth century would probably have been aghast. Do we think that our approach to God in worship is based on anything we can present to him? It is a true principle of all religion, and not just the religion of the Reformers, that we all stand naked and ashamed before God, unable to make any claim on him because of anything we give, or do, or are. We come as receivers, not givers. We come to receive the word of God and the life of God in bread and wine.

Yet even the Reformers could not destroy the tension between giving and receiving. We cannot become capable of receiving except as we give. Our little offerings are an acted sign of our willingness to give all - not to bribe God, not for his sake, not to persuade him that we deserve anything. We must surrender all in order to receive all back, transfigured by its consecration in an ineffable manner. What happens to the bread and wine is not some unnatural marvel. God matches the consecration of the elements with the consecration of the offerers. The earthen vessels must be held up to receive the treasure.

Creeds

Acts 14.23 The Lord in whom they believed.

In the liturgy we often use creeds. But perhaps we misuse them, too. We are worshipping, not disputing, and so we are not concerned on these occasions with dogmatic propositions. We are staking our lives on what we proclaim. We are concerned with committing ourselves to God, Father, Son and Holy Spirit.

Each worshipper is saying: 'I trust myself to God. I stake my life that he is my Father. I risk all to serve his Son. I rely absolutely on the help of the Holy Spirit. I so believe in the church which he has created that I will set about making it what it ought to be, the earthly token of that greater communion of saints which reaches to heaven.'

That is a sketch of what we mean when we use the creeds in worship. We not only hold that they are true; we commit ourselves to those truths, making them the basis of our lives, and letting them re-make us for God's service. We must never be satisfied until we have made each clause alive to us. Here are the truths of spiritual life. We don't create those truths by declaring them. Our disbelief would not change God. But if our lives deny those truths, our spirits cannot thrive.

Deserving

Matthew 20.15 Do you begrudge my generosity?

A parable of Jesus is always about something which doesn't feature in the parable itself. The parable of the lost sheep isn't about sheep, or the parable of the lost coin about money.

So the parable of the labourers in the vineyard isn't about labour relations. Like all the parables, it begins with ordinary everyday things but its meaning depends on its oddity. It is a 'just not so story'. The kingdom of God is not like our everyday lives. No employer acted like that when Jesus told the story, any more than today. God has his own strange ways, choosing to bless good and bad alike, and to reward those who look deserving and those who don't.

The disciples of Jesus hoped for preferential treatment, and they had to learn that they should be happy to see others equally blessed, however much or little they had done to deserve it. And if God was like that, that was what they were to be like, too.

We probably agree that we ought to treat children in that way, giving them what they need or what they will enjoy rather than what they have deserved. But where should we stop applying the rule of need and enjoyment? Why did the Victorians invent a category of 'the deserving poor'?

Differences

John 15.16 You did not choose me.

Unity begins at home. It begins with you and me and my neighbour in the pew. It begins with the conviction that the church is not just a place you go to (or stay away from). The church is people, and those people are conscripts ('You did not choose me, but I chose you'), people called up by God and drafted to a regiment not of their own choosing. We have no right to criticize God's choice of our companions or to let ourselves think that the church would be better without some of its members who don't happen to be our sort.

Once we have ruled out any idea that some people (including ourselves, of course) have more right to be members of the church than others, we must try to realise that each member has something to give to the fellowship. We must start looking for things in others which we do not ourselves possess.

Unity does not come from trying to make everybody alike. It comes when we enjoy our differences, yet realise that we have one shared task: to bring all life into subjection to Christ - the life of the home, the life of work, the life of leisure, science, arts, industry, the life of Britain, of Europe, of the world, all peoples, all things. What a task! How ridiculous to be disunited!

Faith

> Hebrews 11.1. Faith is the substance of things hoped for, the evidence of things not seen.

Faith is neither believing something in the face of evidence nor believing something for which there is no evidence. It is a relationship of trust in a person and self-committal to that person. That kind of faith gives heart to hope and assurance to belief, says the writer to the Hebrews. But the kind of hope or belief it assures depends upon the character of the person.

Take a human analogy. Suppose I have a close and trusted friend and he has asked me to meet him for dinner somewhere. I know him so well that his character is clear to me. He is a good judge of food and wine; and he is habitually unpunctual. I cannot hope that he will arrive on time. But I have every reason to hope that it will be a good meal. The same relationship makes one hope substantial and cuts away the ground from beneath the other.

Faith in God gives heart to the hopes and assurance to the beliefs which are agreeable with the divine nature, and no others. The text gives no grounds for hoping for our heart's desire, whatever that is, nor for believing what we think nicest to believe. Faith brings all hopes and beliefs into the presence of God. There they are denied or confirmed or refined.

Forgiveness

Jeremiah 18.4 The vessel he was making of clay was spoiled, and he reworked it into another vessel.

Forgiveness is a word it's easy to misunderstand. If someone publishes a malicious libel against me, I might say, Never mind, he couldn't help it. It was his heredity or his environment that made him do it. That's magnanimous, but not forgiving. I might say, I'll make him suffer for his wickedness. Then I rescue justice and uphold the moral law, but I'm not forgiving. If I just wish it hadn't happened, I'm trying to run the film of life back through the projector and restore the status quo. Even if I could, still I wouldn't be forgiving.

Evil actions are not just events in time and space, so that one can say, This was done then and there. If so, there would be no need of forgiveness, because time moves on and with its moving the ill would cease to be. The evil actions of men and women are inscribed on their spirits and on the lives of others. That record can't simply be rubbed out. If there is to be a new beginning, it must be made with what already is, with human lives already distorted.

It's something like Jeremiah's picture of the potter re-using old material. Yet that is too peaceful. Forgiveness is costly. We have to kill our strong instinct of self-preservation. It is a kind of death. It is a cross.

Foundations

Matthew 7.24 What then of the man who hears these words of mine and acts upon them?

Probably few of us have ever so much as seen the foundations on which our houses are built. They may have been laid a long time ago. Yet there is nothing about a house which matters so much. If they are insecure, the whole building is in constant peril.

So much for our houses. What about our homes? With many of us it is just as true that their foundations were laid years and years ago. Have we ever inspected them since then, or just forgotten about them as we forget about the foundations of our houses until something goes wrong and the whole house is threatened because its foundations are insecure?

Jesus spoke of the ingredients which go to make secure foundations. In concrete foundations there are two ingredients: cement and ballast, making a hard-setting foundation for building. The two ingredients which Jesus mentioned were hearing his words and doing them.

One recipe for suitable concrete is one part of Portland cement and six parts of river ballast. That may be a parable for the seven days of the week - one for hearing and six for doing. Of course, we don't cut up the week just like that, but it's a good proportion. Listen carefully; but spend most of your life doing.

Freedom

Galatians 4.19 Until Christ be formed in you.

Paul's attitude to his converts poses the great question for parents and teachers, too: are my children 'taking the shape of Christ'?

That great question will raise many others. Can we know what Christ was like? Can we trust the words of the gospels? Must children, like Jesus, be 'subject to' their parents? Will they, too, have to 'learn obedience by the things they suffer'? These are all real questions; but they must not be used to evade the great question.

Clearly children are not to be formed in the shape of a first-century Jewish boy called Jesus. They are to take the form of Christ, that is, to take from the historical Jesus whatever is universal, the maturity of his manhood. That means to discover the freedom he gives, freedom from all bondages, whether to rules and precepts or to the wisdom of the past or to convention, which is the formalized force of other people's opinions. These may all be good things in their right place, yet Jesus was free in relation to them, free to use them without being used by them, free to value the past while pressing on to a new future. That Christ is to be formed in Christian children - and their teachers and parents.

Friendship

III John 14.   Face to face.

There isn't much in the New Testament about one of the great blessings of human life - friendship. But the third letter of John is instinct with the warmth of friendship - There we read, 'I had much to write to you, but I would rather not write with pen and ink; I hope to see you soon, and we will talk together face to face.'

Friends often feel there is so much to say, yet thoughts are too delicate or too complex or too indefinable to be clothed in the written word. They need the extra help of tones of voice, expressions of face, the look of the eyes.

One of the most astonishing things the Bible says about Moses is that the Lord spoke to him face to face, as a man speaks to his friend. This is surely the highest point of prayer. There can never quite be an end of reverence and fear, of breathless awe in the presence of the glory of holiness. But it will be shot through with something else which the New Testament calls 'boldness' or 'freedom of access', a kind of free-speaking encouraged by love. Even as we take the first steps along the road to those heights we already begin to sense the wonder of friendship, the joy of being face to face.

Gentleness

Colossians 4.14   Luke the beloved physician.

The stories and details we find in Luke's gospel but not in the other three seem to have a special character - the birth stories, the parables of the good Samaritan and the prodigal son, the word of forgiveness from the cross, and many another. If we wonder what God is like and then turn to Luke to find out, we learn that he is gentle and merciful, loving the weak and the wayward and the outcast. It is easy to believe that the 'beloved physician' treasured these items because in him God's Holy Spirit had begun to make a copy of the human character of his master.

We know how well such a character would fit in with the calling of a doctor. It was all the more so in a past age when medical science was in its infancy, and so often there was little a physician could do except provide palliatives for diseases which were as yet incurable - little except hold the patients' hands and suffer with them as they groped their way through the valley of the shadow of death. But that gentleness was united with courage - conviction and courage to befriend the despised and champion the outcast.

Every society has its scapegoats. To champion them demands great humility and a gentle spirit, and courage out of the ordinary.

Gifts

Matthew 25.15 To one he gave five talents, to another two, to another one.

Windmills in a landscape were once an everyday thing. Now in just a few places in our country we can see the majestic steady movement of the sweeps, with white sails against a blue sky. How, we may wonder, would Jesus have used that picture in a parable?

Perhaps he would have spoken of the invisible power of the spirit, the wind blowing where it wills and driving the machinery of love in human lives. Perhaps he would have spoken of the clean and free power of the wind, and reproved this generation for abandoning its generosity for the smoke and pollution of fossil fuels, throwing away what is good because we think we have found something better.

Comparing those possible parables, do we suppose that one of them is more spiritual than the other? Is the pentecostal message more religious than the ecological? We are too good at spiritualising our religion. Take, for example, our use of the word 'talent'. In the gospel parable there is no equation between the talents and 'spiritual gifts'. We should include our stewardship of all good things: the good earth, the clean sky, the powerful winds and tides, and all God's creatures.

Glory

John 17.22 The glory which you have given me I have given to them.

Suppose we are in a dark building, perhaps an old church. It is a cloudless day and the sun is shining with all its power. If we try to look out of the window directly at the sun, we shall be dazzled. It is too bright for our eyes. If we stand back in the shadow, however, we can see the shaft of light which streams in through the window. But clearest of all will be the light reflected from some bright object - a polished metal cross, perhaps, or a brass memorial.

It is a common experience. Perhaps it is like our experience of God. We can't see him as he is. We can't bear the splendour of his glory, like the sun in a cloudless sky. The splendour of light hides him. We can, however, see light coming forth from light, the glory of God in the face of Jesus Christ, the light of the world. And we can see the Holy Spirit of God at work in those who reflect that light. Courage, self-sacrifice, forgiveness, love, joy, peace - there we see the reflected light shining in other men and women.

Jesus said, I am the light of the world. He also said, You are the light of the world. The glory which had been given to him, he gave to others. He came to light the glory of the Father in us.

Guidance

I Corinthians 7.40 I think that I have the spirit of God.

The promise of the gospel is that the guidance of God's Holy Spirit is available to every individual Christian. With the coming of Christ there came into force that new covenant which had been foretold by Jeremiah. No-one any longer should say to a neighbour, Know the Lord. For they would all know God, from the least to the greatest.

According to the second chapter of Acts, Peter claimed that the prophecy of Joel had been fulfilled, the prophecy that God would pour out his spirit on all flesh. The gospel is about the abolition of an outward law and the gift of an inward guiding spirit.

The church as a whole has a duty to advise and persuade. But personal decisions rest properly with the conscience of the individual. It would perhaps be easier if we could go to some fount of authority and receive our decisions ready-made. But that may not be. The individual cannot escape responsibilities.

The first responsibility is to educate one's own conscience. That is done chiefly by listening, perhaps to the voices of the world, but above all within the fellowship of Christian people, till one can say with Paul, I think that I have the spirit of God.

Holiness

Matthew 6.9 Hallowed be your name.

Holiness in the Bible is not only strange and fascinating. It also evokes fear. Abram experienced a horror of great darkness, the disciples on the mount of transfiguration are afraid, and perhaps even Jesus in Gethsemane experienced something of this fear which the holiness of God cannot help arousing in the human mind.

Where is the place for the hallowing of God's name in the modern western world? In past ages men and women most often came into contact with holiness through nature, through holy people and places, or through the general mystery of life and of the world. Today many, perhaps most, of us never come into contact with nature except in a tamed and domesticated form. Since the dissolution of the monasteries we have almost eliminated recognizably holy men and women and turned holy places into sight-seeing attractions. We are busy depriving the world of most of its mysteriousness through science.

Holiness has been shut out of normal experience. No wonder that we can only understand the holiness of God in terms of righteousness and justice. Religion has come to mean doing good and nothing more. We need to get holiness back into our worship - even perhaps a little fear.

Humanity

Romans 12.1 Present your bodies as a living sacrifice.

In humanity the worship of the created order attains consciousness. There may be some mystical, inexpressible sense in which all creation worships its maker, but, as the Psalmist says, in all except humanity 'there is neither speech nor language'.

We may sympathize with Walt Whitman's praise of animals because
They do not sweat and whine about their condition,
They do not lie awake in the dark and weep for their sins.

But the heights and depths are linked, the deep oceans imply the high himalayas. Our miserable sycophancy is the inverse of our ability to be caught up into the highest heavens.

In our worship, however, we can only offer ourselves, not some distilled humanity, colourless and featureless, but beings of such hopes and potentialities, compounded of fierce desires and appetites, of such potential joys and sorrows. We are like that. That is how he has made us. When we worship there must be the oblation of the hard actuality of our human nature, with our possessions and our communities.

It would vitiate our worship if we thought we should offer an ethereal, disembodied nature. God could have made us, like himself, 'without body, parts or passions'. He did not.

Hypocrisy

Luke 12.1 Beware of the leaven of the Pharisees, which is hypocrisy.

People often misunderstand the meaning of hypocrisy. They suppose it means conscious insincerity - using words, performing actions, which we ourselves know to be insincere. If that were all it meant, there would be no need to worry about it unduly.

The sin of hypocrisy is more subtle. It depends on submerging self-knowledge just below the level of awareness. It is a kind of deliberate forgetfulness, like the behaviour of the man with faith but no works, in the Epistle of James, who looks in the mirror and goes away and 'forgets' what he is like. Hypocrisy involves conniving at our own forgetfulness, encouraging ourselves to forget, taking no steps to remind ourselves what kind of people we are. To be reminded, we need friends. We need at least someone who loves us enough to tell us the truth, and whom we love enough to listen - and still remain friends.

Is it significant that in the New Testament the word hypocrisy is confined to the gospels? Did the first Christians quickly forget how often Jesus had pointed to hypocrisy as the besetting sin of religious people? It can't survive alongside true self-knowledge. So we must pray, Lord, help us to know ourselves.

Imagination

Philippians 1.18 In pretence or sincerity, Christ is proclaimed.

Nobody knows what Jesus looked like. Nobody knows what Peter or John looked like. There are some traditional ways of representing their appearance. But they have no historical basis. For all we know Peter might have been a wizened little man and John a burly six-footer. And if Jesus was hump-backed and had a cast in one eye, it might offend against our feelings of reverence, but it can't be said to go against the evidence.

There is a problem here. The story of the Gospels may mean little to us unless it is brought alive and made contemporary, through the use of imagination - ours or someone else's. In that way it can speak to us, challenge us, change us. We may see things clearly - but not as they actually were. One 'Life of Jesus' portrays him as a workers' leader and revolutionary. Is that a good portrait? What about Godspell and Jesus Christ Superstar?

Paul wrote, 'What does it matter? One way or another, in pretence or sincerity, Christ is set forth, and for that I rejoice.' We don't have to be protective about Jesus Christ. If we want a churchly monopoly of him, it may be because we secretly want to protect our own cosy world from the disruptive effect of his person and his teaching.

Inheritance

Deuteronomy 6.12 Take heed lest you forget the Lord.

There they were, the ancient Israelites, with their God-given cities and wells and vineyards - and in danger of forgetting God. Perhaps they might do it by becoming so much enamoured of the gifts that they just pushed the giver out of their thoughts. But perhaps they might forget God by supposing that it was their own strength and skill that had obtained them, and therefore, as mere man-made possessions, they could be changed or destroyed without a second thought, and certainly without account rendered to God.

In the church we, too, may forget God. We may become so concerned about our inheritance (music, architecture, an 'incomparable liturgy') that we forget whose glory they are meant to serve. Or else we may forget that we are stewards accountable to God for what we have received - our particular suburb of the city of God, which we have not built, our particular well of salvation which we did not dig, our patch of vines or olives which we did not plant.

We dare not claim a free hand to change it all or destroy it. If we stand in the ruins of a monastery today, we can see that it has happened in the past. Are we less arrogant than the Tudors?

Justice

Psalm 82.3 Give justice to the weak.

The word justice sounds like something unalterable. Surely, we say, here is something that doesn't change. How wrong we are. No doubt there is an unchanging heart to it. It means giving everyone his due. It always means that. But what exactly is due to each one?

Ideas about that are always changing. In feudal times each one's due was reckoned according to rank. The lord's due and the serf's due were two quite different things. In this age our attention has been drawn to the difference between what society thinks is man's due and what it thinks is woman's due. And all kinds of groups, from small groups of workers up to whole nations and even groups of nations, are simply refusing to accept the idea of their 'due' which has been imposed on them. They say Yes to the idea of justice, and No to the version of it which has been widely held in the past. Why, they ask, should we be poorer, suffer more social handicap, be regarded as inferior, have less say in decisions that affect us, than others who are no more necessary to social life than we are?

I need to learn that justice for others must mean sacrifice for me.

Kingdom

John 18.36 My kingdom is not of this world.

In the teaching of Jesus the idea of the kingdom crops up more often than the idea of love. God has a secret kingdom which you can enter without moving an inch. It is 'at hand'. It is growing secretly. It is a hidden treasure. It was specially active in the life and ministry of Jesus. But although in one sense it was really there, the disciples were to pray that it would come. Their fellowship was an inescapable signal of God's kingship, a flag nailed to the mast. It is a wonderfully rich image. It is the very warp on which all Jesus' other teaching is woven.

We must not get it confused with a decent comfortable life in prosperous western society. Its denizens are the poor, the mourners, the meek, the hungry and thirsty, the merciful, the pure in heart, the peacemakers, the persecuted. Theirs is the kingdom.

And who does our society admire? The rich, the healthy, the successful, the well-off, the competitive, the liberated, the confronters, the dominant. If you turn each of the Beatitudes upside down, you have portraits of the heroes and heroines of the kingdom of this world. It is a revolutionary act to pray, Thy kingdom come.

Maturity

I Corinthians 3.1 Infants in Christ.

Paul told the Corinthian Christians that he had to treat them like babies. The contrast between the two stages of infancy and maturity in faith is paralleled elsewhere in his writings by the contrast between the natural and the spiritual man.

The criterion by which we can test our maturity, or spirituality, is simply the test of unity. 'While there is jealousy and strife among you, you are living on the purely human level of your lower nature.' These things betray the infantile status of so-called Christians. And this does not refer simply to strife of a petty or personal nature; it includes conflict arising from allegiance to different leaders and teachers - saying 'I am Paul's man' or 'I am for Apollos'.

Do we take his teaching seriously? It seems plain that we can never excuse our rivalries by saying that they are founded on genuine convictions. Where they are allowed to separate those who acknowledge the same Lord they reduce adults to the level of children and spiritual beings to the level of the merely human or carnal. So we get the strange paradox that we can become so committed to one version of Christian doctrine that it ceases to have any spiritual value for us.

Meeting

Revelation 2.10 Be faithful unto death and I will give you the crown of life.

When we meet people, we don't stop to analyse what's going on between us. If we did, we might picture it as the confrontation of two independent wills. There may be co-operation, or there may be resistance. The other person makes demands on us, if only to recognise his or her freedom. If those demands are met, we can unite to achieve what neither of us can do separately.

That is true in a much higher degree of any meeting with God. There is no limit to his demands, nor any limit to his help once those demands are acknowledged.

This is to talk in the abstract, and most of us find abstract thinking difficult. So God embodied this truth - incarnated it in Jesus Christ. He makes demands without limit. He makes no apologetic request for discipleship. He demands with an authority which would be fanatical if he were just a man. But if he demands all, he offers all. He will be with us to the end of the world. His spirit will be our strengthener and will never desert us. See his response to the continual calls of human need, and you see on the plane of humanity the limitless self-giving of God. He calls us to be faithful unto death; and in his own death he releases the power which can keep us faithful.

Mystery

Psalm 139.14 I am fearfully and wonderfully made.

In worship we stand humbly before the mystery of Deity. But there is something strangely insensitive about us if we never stand in awe before the lesser mystery of our own Humanity. Have we never felt a sense of amazement at some great work of art, at the prodigious genius of the young Mozart or the prodigal invention of the mature Shakespeare? Have we never felt at a loss as we try to comprehend the intellectual mastery of some great scientist? Have we not admired without understanding the gifts of the Spirit shown in lives of other men and women, courage more than we had dreamed of, love stronger than we can conceive, gifts of healing, of sympathy, of self-sacrifice that are beyond our spiritual horizons? And along with a feeling of discouragement there is a kind of pride, as we remember that these are human beings - and we are human too.

There is a majesty and a mystery about humanity. We are even a mystery to ourselves. We can surprise ourselves at times, as we look back and wonder at what we have been able to do, to say, to think, to suffer. Then perhaps we remember the words of the Psalm, and bow before the Maker of our own mystery.

Neighbours

Matthew 22.39 You shall love your neighbour as yourself.

Sometimes it can be a depressing experience to study the faces of a crowd of people. You see long faces and broad faces, dark faces and fair faces, young faces and old faces. Some bear the marks of greed or self-indulgence; others show the signs of pride and a critical spirit. Scarcely among them all will you see one that is gentle and compassionate, tender and self-forgetful.

You may find yourself echoing the mocking words of Sir Walter Raleigh, the man of letters, who wrote:

I wish I loved the human race.
I wish I loved its silly face.

Loving the human race is both too hard and too easy. If it involves a sentiment of general amiability towards mankind, we can all do that from an armchair. Nothing is easier. But if it involves a deep concern and a personal responsibility for every single member of the human race, it is utterly impossible. And so Jesus did not say, Love mankind. But he did say, Love your neighbour as yourself.

How do you treat yourself? When you're criticized, do you make excuses? Then do so for others. When you're in difficulties, do you welcome help from someone else? Then give it to others. Get out of the armchair. Love some of those anxious faces

Newness

Ephesians 2.15 A single new humanity.

God is, in the view of the biblical writers, concerned with newness. 'Behold, I make all things new' is just a summary of many other passages to the same effect.

It may come as rather a shock. We are more used to the idea that God is the same yesterday, today and for ever. We find great comfort in the changelessness of God, and suppose that he wants things to stay the same.

Perhaps that's one thing that's wrong with the church. Instead of newness, we want renewal, reformation, restoration, returning to the past. If so, that doesn't match the promise and the demand of the gospel which speaks of new wine, a new commandment, a new covenant, new doctrine.

There really are new things, in technology for instance - the microchip, space exploration, organ transplants, and so on. God always had them, as it were, up his sleeve, but at a particular moment they appeared, and their appearance reverberated through human society. We can also think of new things in our own lives. Once we couldn't speak, once we couldn't read, once we hadn't found our faith. These really new things left nothing else just as it was before.

And a new community? Christ's purpose is to break down walls of hostility, to create a new community based on mutual love. And peace at last.

Non-attachment

I Corinthians 7.30 Let those who buy live as though they had no goods.

Property is a problem. The happy picture of communism in the early church soon has a dark shadow thrown across it by the episode of Ananaias and Sapphira who withhold some of their property, and fall dead. In one of his parables Jesus included property among the things which prevent men (and it actually is men, not women) from answering God's invitation to his banquet.

But we all seem pretty much at home in a property-owning democracy. On a larger scale, national sovereignty includes a claim to own particular stretches of the earth's surface, and the air above it, and the minerals below it. The world is full of death and misery because of the conflicts which arise from disputed possessions.

The Old Testament may offer an ideal of 'every man under his vine and under his fig tree', but the New Testament offers a model of communism, of non-possession; and the patterns of community most frequently followed in Christian history have been of non-possession, of 'holy poverty'.

When Paul counsels an attitude of non-attachment it is, he thinks, on the eve of doomsday, but our frail grasp on life itself makes that attitude just as suitable for us all. The unity of mankind is threatened by possessiveness - and the unity of Christian people.

Opportunities

Ephesians 5.16 Redeeming the time.

Buy up your opportunities, says the text. Isn't that bitter advice! Aren't we all conscious of opportunities lost, the kind word unspoken, the helping action left undone? But does it mean that we have to spend our time anxiously watching and waiting, like a photographer with his finger on the shutter release, poised for the exact moment in a rapid action or the fleeting expression on a child's face? Is life to be like that, with one's nerves continually on edge?

If we ask such questions, it shows that we are acting the part of Christians, not living the life of Christ. In the gospels we can see how no question left Jesus perplexed, no situation found him at a loss. He was not calculating the effect of his words or actions. For him, there was no conflict between what he ought to do and what he wanted to do. His actions and words were perfectly natural and at the same time perfectly loving, because love was his nature.

Sometimes we meet other people who are, in their degree, like him. It is because the eternal Christ lives in them. Only beginners have to buy up their opportunities.

Pleasure

Revelation 4.11 Thou hast created all things and for thy pleasure they are and were created

The translators of the Authorized Version have given us the idea that all creation is for God's 'pleasure'. It isn't exactly there in the original Greek, but it is an idea worth pursuing.

Our own pleasures are often mere diversions from the serious and exhausting business of earning a living or running a home. But it is absurd to suppose that God, the source of all life, needs recuperation. Nor can we suppose that he looks on the teeming world and the mass of humanity as entertaining toys for the amusement of his idle moments.

Instead we should think of the pleasure of an artist or craftsman in what he is making - the painting or the sculpture or the piece of furniture or the garden that takes up his attention. It has no reason to exist except the pleasure of its creator. If he did not choose to make it, it would never come to be.

We, too, tiny bits of the created universe, would never have come into existence if God had not been pleased to make us. If we can't face the fact of our contingency, then true religion will for ever be unknown to us. We must begin with humility before God who created all things for his pleasure.

Possessions

I Timothy 4.4 Nothing is to be rejected if it is received with thanksgiving.

Look at life in a suburb. Its inhabitants are clearly pre-occupied with material possessions. Is that a good thing? Part of the answer is that God may be calling those men and women to renounce possessions for the sake of his Kingdom. But there is another side to the teaching of the Bible. Its good characters are not always poor. Material wealth is sometimes recognised as God's gift, even in the New Testament. Would God have created so rich and fertile a world or men with such inventive ingenuity if he had not intended us to enjoy the riches of the world and the fruits of human ingenuity? There is some nonsense talked about materialism. Perhaps a parent wants more money to give the children better food and clothing. Perhaps a woman wants domestic appliances to have more time to be a good neighbour. There is no materialism when possessions are wanted in order to change human relations for the better. So there is a tug-of-war. Two thoughts wrestle for mastery in our minds: suspicion of the allurements of money and belief that all good things come from God. If the second thought wins we must sanitize it with thanksgiving. But it is better to let the wrestling match go on.

Principles

Matthew 11.16   Children sitting in the market places

We all know the petulant cry of disagreeable children, 'Well I won't play then!'. If they don't get their own way, they won't do what someone else suggests. It was just the same in Palestine two thousand years ago. And the disciples remembered Jesus saying that adults were like that, too. John the Baptist had given them the example of a stern, ascetic life of self-denial, and they wouldn't imitate him. Jesus himself had led a sociable life, sharing innocent pleasures and mixing with those who wanted to enjoy themselves, and they wouldn't follow him either.

At least with children it often happens that a group who are quarreling at one moment are playing happily together five minutes later. But grown-ups (as we call them) are quite capable of erecting a mood into a principle and justifying their stubbornness by high-sounding arguments. John the ascetic is accused of being mad. Jesus the friend of pleasure-seekers is accused of being self-indulgent.

We must always question any argument which conveniently excuses us from changing our life-style and take a hard look at anything we call 'a matter of principle'.

Religion

Acts 17.22 In every way you are very religious.

Is religion a good thing? Christians threaten each other with murder in Northern Ireland, and elsewhere Muslims and Sikhs and Hindus are at each other's throats. There are plenty of people who would loudly answer, No! And that answer would be based, not on arguments and ideas, but on bitter personal experience of the suffering it has brought.

Paul said the people of Athens were very religious. For all that, he believed God was unknown to them. So he tried to do two things. First, he tried to detach them from allegiance to the beautiful temples and chiselled shrines which graced the Acropolis. If there was any sense in asking, Where is God? the answer could only be, In him we live and move and have our being. The second thing was to tell them that God had revealed himself in a particular human life, the life of the man Jesus, and that all religion was to be judged by the standard of that life.

Is our religion a good thing? Only if we remember that it is people who make up the temple of God's presence, not buildings, however venerable; and that all religion is to be tested by the standard of Christ's life. By that standard much that calls itself Christianity fails. Much that is called by some other name passes the test.

Rest

Exodus 20.8 Remember the sabbath day.

Man does not live by work alone - nor woman neither. That principle underlies the sabbath commandment. There must be a place for other things beside work, as no doubt the atheist would agree. The distinctiveness of Christianity consists in what it has to say about those other things. Not by bread alone, said Jesus, - that is, not just by the products of labour - but by every word of God - that is, by his words of command, his words of comfort, his words of gracious loving-kindness, and above all his words of creation.

We have to work to satisfy our needs, but the fulness of life can't be earned. It has to be given, and received as a gracious gift. The real meaning of the sabbath commandment is that we need to rest from busy activity in order that we may rest in God and in what he has created and called good.

One way to do that is in worship. But the unearned treasure of life is not locked up in church or confined to one day a week. As leisure increases we have more opportunities for resting in God and his works. There are a thousand ways in which we can begin to understand what it means in Genesis when it says that God saw everything he had made and, behold, it was very good.

Rules

Matthew 5.18 Till all be fulfilled

God's people in Old Testament times were given rules to obey, whether or not they understood the reasons for them. God's will was often mysterious and unaccountable. His ways were not their ways nor his thoughts their thoughts. Their duty was to obey. But as they obeyed, they discovered the joy of obedience and came to love him whom they obeyed. 'I have had as great delight in thy commandments as in all manner of riches.'

At that point obedience was swallowed up in love, and the law was fulfilled. In religion it is always true that each particular regulation is fulfilled as its real meaning and purpose is seen, understood, accepted. Up to that point the command has binding force. After that it is unnecessary. It may actually become a hindrance to true spiritual growth, keeping enslaved those who are meant to be free.

We are constrained by love, acting as children who delight to please their father, not bound by rules and regulations as though we were unwilling servants. But sometimes those very rules can still be the means by which we express our love.

Sanctification

I Thessalonians 4.3 This is the will of God, even your sanctification.

Think of the course of a normal Christian life. It has its beginning and its end. The beginning is marked by baptism, whether this happens in childhood or maturity. That is the point at which we claim for ourselves or have claimed for us a place within God's covenant people, his holy people, the church of Jesus Christ. The end is what the Bible calls our perfection, the point at which God has so worked upon the human spirit as to banish forever the workings of sin.

Between that beginning and that end, somewhere or other, there is an important change. It is what Paul seems to mean by sanctification. We can sometimes recognise it in people we meet. It isn't easy to describe, but perhaps we can say that it means losing the desire to sin: no longer wanting to use hurtful words, no longer wanting to show that we are better than other people, no longer wanting to 'get our own back'. It may still happen that sin, so to speak, breaks in and has its way momentarily. But the sanctified person hates sin, repudiates it, disowns it, even in the moment when it is mastering him.

We know people like that - not yet perfect, mind you, but already sanctified. It can happen to anyone.

Seeing

Mark 8.24 I see men as trees walking.

We have all seen an old painting of a horse race or a hunting scene in which the artist drew the galloping horses with their legs sticking out fore and aft, almost horizontally. They drew them like that because they saw them like that. In fact, they saw something that wasn't there. High speed photography has proved that horses don't gallop like that.

A parable lurks here. We distort what we see in the moment of seeing - not just horses galloping, but the things of the spirit. We look out through windows hung with cobwebs - prejudice, cowardice, sloth, to name a few. Now we see much of the world through a television screen; it comes to us as 'news'. Truth begins at the sub-editor's desk.

Evelyn Underhill once wrote that to see the world spiritually we need a veritable spring-cleaning of the soul. We must get rid of the cobwebs, perhaps replace the distorting glass in our windows.

Paul wrote of 'discerning spiritually'. We might take that to mean a way, not just of discriminating, but actually of looking. Jesus has taught us that the real world is the world where the widow's mite is of greater value than large offerings made out of abundance, where the humble sinner is nearer God than the proud Pharisee, where the penitent dying thief is at the doorstep of paradise. We must learn to see that real world.

Self-realisation

Colossians 2.10 You are complete in him.

In the discreditable story of David's adultery and murder in II Samuel 11 we read that he asked Uriah 'how Joab was doing and how the people fared, and how the war prospered'. Or so it appears in our versions. But if those questions had been quite literally translated we should find David asking 'after the peace of Joab and the peace of the people and the peace of the war'.

David wasn't specially interested in peace for its own sake; he spent much of his time fighting. He meant 'Has Joab got what he wanted (glory) and the people what they wanted (loot) and is the war perfect (a good scrap)'. The leading idea of the Hebrew word for peace (Shalom) is completeness.

Peace is having everything our nature requires. It is what we call nowadays self-realization. Everybody wants it. To the warmonger there is no peace except war. To the hard business executive peace means the liquidation of all competitors. The ideological fanatic can find no peace except by choking other people's ideas. It depends on what they think is the true nature of humankind.

The Christian sees it only in Jesus Christ. He is the Prince of Peace. Or, as Paul says, we are complete in him.

Sensitivity

Ephesians 4.19   Being past feeling.

We are creatures of shifting moods and fluctuating emotions. A mature religion, therefore, cannot depend on religious feelings. Salvation is not a matter of feelings, but of status. It is what God has done for us, not our sense of it. God has redeemed the world through Christ. Our emotional response can neither create nor destroy what God has done.

It would be curious if I asked myself, 'Do I feel British this morning?'. My nationality is a status resulting from past events. Nor should I say, 'Do I feel like a justified sinner?'. That is my status, because of the events I recount when I say the creed.

But though salvation is not dependent on feelings, right conduct usually is. For that we need quick, responsive feelings. Mrs Bennet, in *Pride and Prejudice*, declares that, if it were not for the entail, she would not mind anything at all. Mr Bennet gravely replies, 'Let us be thankful that you are preserved from a state of such insensibility.'

Be thankful for sensibility. Because those who are past feeling give themselves over to sin, we need to cultivate the utmost sensitivity towards each other. The degradation of sin is to be past feeling. Part of the glory of the Son of Man was tender sympathy.

Singing

Colossians 3.16 Teaching and admonishing one another in psalms and hymns and spiritual songs.

Worshippers are sometimes strangely reluctant to sing. Giving out a hymn number ought to be like breaking the wires on a bottle of champagne - the prelude to bubbling over. But it often seems that the fermentation hasn't generated enough pressure.

We need to be clear what we are doing. Paul says that we sing with grace in our hearts, that is, out of thankfulness and by the moving of God's own freely given spirit. Psalms and hymns are offerings of worship. But before mentioning that rather obvious truth, he says that we sing in order to teach and admonish one another.

That throws some light on the general method of Christian learning. It is not by propositional instruction, as though there were some kind of Christian Euclid to be got by heart. It is by putting ourselves into a current of life, a continuously flowing stream of shared experience. That is, after all, much what the communion of saints means - fellowship in experience with the disciples of every age.

Only a misplaced egoism can demand that every word of a hymn or psalm is directly relevant to my own individual experience. I can sing words not tailor-made for me, and discover in hymnody a sacrament of unity.

Spirit

Matthew 6.9 Pray like this.

Give us this day our daily bread - that is the prayer of Adam in the Garden of Eden, man unfallen, man nevertheless dependent on powers he did not create, helpless without the bounty of the natural world.

But in the Lord's Prayer we move on, with the word 'forgive' to a different relationship, that of a sinner to his redeemer, Adam out of paradise, beyond the barrier of the flaming sword. By confession comes forgiveness.

Then the pattern prayer leads our thoughts outward, to the world we must forgive, the world where temptation will be met and evil must be conquered. So confession leads to reconciling service in the world.

It seems that so far in the Lord's Prayer we have honoured the Father and the redeeming Son. But what of the Holy Spirit? It is he who has moved our hearts to prayer; and he involves us in a corporate act, a unifying act. Worship draws us together into one body, governed by one spirit.

This is a splendid vision, yet it can be cruelly mocked by experience if the unity of worship is splintered by overgrown individualism. If our own preferences are not met, our own prejudices are unsatisfied, we can become, not worshippers, but critics, spectators not suppliants. To pray the Lord's prayer we must let the Holy Spirit exorcize our self-regard.

Suffering

Matthew 5.5 They shall inherit the earth.

If there is good news for a suffering world, it is that God enters it to redeem it, so that a new glory shines and transfigures the dark scene. Everyone needs that gospel at certain times.

Yet there is more to life than suffering. For an increasing number of human beings (so we hope) suffering is or will become an occasional, manageable experience. If we know the gospel for the sufferers, what is the gospel for those who don't suffer? Suppose we had given meat to the hungry and drink to the thirsty; suppose we had taken in the stranger, clothed the naked, visited the sick and the prisoners, what would there be to say to those who are none of these?

The church's first response has been to concentrate on the sins of affluence, to say that the gospel offers release from greed, from ruthless competition, from the destructive tension of one-upmanship. Very true. Yet there are those who don't need that gospel either - the meek who are neither sufferers nor worshippers of Mammon.

The answer seems simple. Blessed are the meek, for they shall inherit the earth, this earth, with all its wonders. There must be a gospel of creation which is as important as the gospel of redemption - of enjoyment as well as self-denial; of leisure as well as work.

The Body of Christ

Ephesians 4.12 The body of Christ.

Paul's first experience as a Christian convert, blinded with the splendour of his new-found Lord, was of a voice in which fear wrestled with love, saying to him, the fiercest of persecutors, Brother Saul.

In that word he recognised that God had created a new kinship, of which the bond was not birth nor race nor a code of law nor the rite of circumcision, but simply faith, a living relationship with Christ and through him with all who had been redeemed by the power of the cross.

This new kinship could not be described merely as discipleship of a beloved master. For the person who stood at the centre of this new community was not dead, but alive again from the dead, and so much alive that he was active in all his followers. Their relation with each other was more than the unity of those who shared a common faith. They were so closely knit together that they could be described as the limbs of a spiritual body. This spiritual union was as real as the union of limbs in a material body. And because Christ was pleased to act and proclaim salvation through this fellowship, this community, it was to be described plainly as the body of Christ.

Tradition

Matthew 12.42 A greater than Solomon is here.

King Solomon, we read, made a great collection of wise sayings from the past.

Contrast that painstaking process with the originality of Jesus. He saw himself as the fulfiller, not the destroyer, of traditions. Yet he is marked off from all the ponderous Solomons of this world by two things.

First, he claimed freedom to use tradition creatively. All that the past had to offer must be made to subserve the future. That future was the reign of God in which the sabbath was made for man, not man for the sabbath. There was much to learn from the wisdom of the past, but in the last analysis it was like old wineskins which could not hold the new wine of the kingdom.

The second difference was that Jesus trusted his hearers to make their own choices. We know the finger-wagging tone of the Book of Proverbs. My son, do this. My son, keep clear of that. Jesus challenges men and women to make their own choices. He says outrageous things to force people to wake up and think. Hate your father and mother. Sell everything. Cut off your hand. Dig out your eye. He constantly asks questions. What do you think? How can this be? Which do you think is better?

He is greater than Solomon, in not giving all the answers.

Trinity

Ephesians 4.3 The unity of the spirit.

William Langland, the author of Piers Plowman, used a strange image to expound the doctrine of the Holy Trinity - the image of a hand. The Father is like a fist, the Son like the fingers, the Holy Spirit like the palm.

He seems to mean that God the Father, as he is in himself from all eternity, is the power which a clenched fist suggests - God Almighty. The power of the hand is turned into creative activity by the fingers, in painting or drawing or carving. That corresponds to God the Son, coming forth from all eternity in manifold activities of creation and salvation. The palm organizes the action of the separate fingers, and corresponds to the Holy Spirit, the principle of unity.

It is an odd fancy. Yet it can set us thinking, if we believe humanity is made in God's image, and his tri-une nature is the pattern for human communities. They embody power, like the fist. That power finds expression in many ways, like the activities of the fingers. And all the time there is a centre of unity. We don't invent it. It's not a philosophy or ideology. It's given by God, there before we search for it, awaiting our discovery, the deep reality of our oneness with each other simply as human beings sharing in the image of God.

Unity

Ephesians 4.5 One Lord, one faith, one baptism.

The well-known hymn by Dean Plumptre says 'We shall maintain unfliching One Church, one Faith, one Lord', Does the truth of Christian unity depends on us? Is it somehow of our creating?

Paul, by contrast, speaks of God's gifts which are there for the asking, and cannot be destroyed by human infidelity, as they certainly were not created by human thought. Again, the hymn puts the church first, uses 'the faith' to mean a body of doctrine, and reaches its climax with 'one Lord', as though the Lord is discovered by accepting that doctrine within that church.

Paul, on the other hand, describes the progress of the human soul - of his own soul. He met the Lord on the Damascus road, made his great act of faith, and owned that faith in asking for baptism.

So there are two ways of speaking about Christian unity. One is to say, Here is the Church; within that Church there is inspired doctrine; and union with the Lord comes by accepting that doctrine within that church. The other way is to say, Unity is here already. It is given to us. Thanks be to God for his unspeakable gift. To whom has the Lord spoken? In whom has he awakened trust? To whom has he given new life in baptism? All such are his. All have one Lord, one faith, one baptism.

Vocation

I Corinthians 7.17. Let everyone lead the life which the Lord has assigned to him, and in which God has called him.

The call, or vocation, of Christ is not to a particular kind of work. Paul wrote about the life in which God has called each one. Note: 'in', not 'to'. The context of life is left undisturbed. The vocation of a disciple is generally to do as a Christian what others do without any thought of God.

There is a spectrum of jobs in which a Christian can fulfil his or her vocation, ranging from those which would not exist apart from Christ (that is, various ministries in his church) through those which we might call secular ministries (in medicine, social work, education and so on) to all those jobs which sustain the fabric of life together (in the home, at work, in the arts, at leisure).

One part of this spectrum is not intrinsically more 'Christian' than another. All that is ruled out is anything destructive of common life (and opinions may differ about what that includes). On the basis of New Testament teaching we can't call some work 'vocational', and then justify lower pay or worse conditions of work in it. Indeed I Timothy 5.17 proposes double pay for teachers and preachers. We can't avoid the risk of railway strikes by asserting that some men (and women?) have a divine calling to drive diesels.

Wisdom

Job 28.12 Where shall wisdom be found?

What is Christian wisdom? Often in the Bible wisdom is a practical gift. It has little to do with speculation, and everything to do with life, with creativeness, with good order, with the service and worship of God.

If trinitarian theology is Christian wisdom, it must address the business of life, rather than the arguments of the lecture-room. It must be lay wisdom, not just clerical wisdom. Even the Athanasian Creed begins by saying that the catholic faith is 'that we worship one God in Trinity and Trinity in Unity' - not that we have certain ideas, but a way of worship.

A trinitarian Christian is one who worships God's creative spirit at work wherever people find unity with each other; who worships God who changed the world by the life, death and triumph of Christ; who worships God as greater than the universe he has made, holding the initiative now, as always. That worship is directed to the single great reality we name as God. It must be the offering of a total life, responding to the presence of God in others, finding Christ as master and friend in daily life, and ready to receive the initiatives of the transcendent God who makes all things new. Such a worshipper is truly wise.

Worship

John 4.23. The true worshippers will worship the Father in spirit and in truth.

The hand for work - the head for wit - the heart for worship. So runs an inscription in a Somerset belfry.

One man has the first two but not the third. In work and wit he is such a one as God meant him to be; yet something is lacking.

Another has something deep in his nature which responds to his Creator and gives honour to his Saviour, a little mirror in his soul which gives back a dim reflection of God's light pouring in. Does he stand mute when hymns are sung? Does he snore while the preacher proses from the pulpit? Never mind; he has a heart for worship, and he is a good disciple of his master.

We may puzzle to know how Jesus who was Emmanuel could need to worship, but there is no denying that he did so. He had a hand for work and a head for wit, and a heart for worship, too. It was not only the nights spent in prayer. It was the way he responded to the revelation of the Father in every flower and every unregarded animal of God's creation. His whole life was worship, for he lived in the light of a presence that was holy and loving, generous and good. Without worship we cannot be whole.

Little Seeds

There can be no love where we refuse to be indebted to others, and stand on our supposed self-sufficiency.

Noone can exercise Christian love alone; it needs a context, a sphere in which to work.

The child is concerned only for itself; the adult is concerned for others as well; the saint only for others.

We may never pray for anything which we can have only by making someone else go without.

When we are faced with what we aren't good enough to do, it is convenient to tell ourselves that we don't want to do it.

The inner conflicts which harass human beings are both the cause of their degradation and the clue to their glory.

The Church has a public life, apparent to all, and a secret life, known only to its members.

Hope, unlike mere optimism, faces the fact that the past and the future will be of the same sort.

Leisure is not time off being a child of God; it sets us free to be what we really are.

It is a good test of Christian character to ask whether a man or woman is less exacting to others than to himself or herself.

We can point to nothing which is ours apart from God.

Church people must always go to outsiders as to men and women who already have access to the same Lord.

Jesus Christ was no less the way, the truth and the life when he was utterly deserted on the cross than when crowds flocked to hear him.

The Christian disciple is free from the tyranny of rules and regulations, but punctilious in those things which express his gratitude to God.

We must ask of every kind of work, Is it fit for the hands of God incarnate?

We have already begun to spend eternity with God.

Sometimes when we are unhappy it is just through forgetfulness.

To believe in providence is not to deny that evil is real; it is to deny that it is final.

The trees of the garden of Eden were, to be sure, good trees, but they came between Adam and God.

In warfare the dividing line between the saved and the damned is never the line of battle.

You can almost tell people's age - you can certainly gauge their attitude to ageing - by noticing whether they welcome or hate new beginnings.

Prayer is not meant to be a substitute for thought and common sense; it prepares the way for them.

We are all constantly editing the Christian faith to suit ourselves.

We can sin by doing nothing.

English people love sport, and think of God as a celestial referee, ready to blow the whistle at the first sign of foul play; they are annoyed when he doesn't.

It cannot be God's will that the rich and varied heritage of the different churches should be bartered away in the name of good-will.

Equal opportunities mislead the simple-minded into supposing that it is somehow wrong to look up to anybody else.

Every time there is some big scientific advance, some Christian somewhere loses what little faith he had.

There are blessings which some people can never have because they themselves are too big.

We can be sure that God will not give other people what he knows is bad for them just because we have mistakenly asked him to do so.

Jesus avoided no customs because they might be abused and no company because it was despised.

All things are either Caesar's or God's; nothing is our own with absolute right of possession.

If we think we are self-made men and women, there is no particular reason why we should not set out to unmake others.

We do not have to try to make our families holy; they are that already, by God's creation.

We can only measure the greatness of St Paul if we can imagine what it is like to find that the bottom has fallen out of life - and then to rise triumphant.

Christians cannot be trusted to support the *status quo;* they are taught, in the Lord's Prayer, to pray for a revolution.

When we go to church, we don't simply stroll along to a venerable building; we go to Mount Sion, the City of the living God.

Let the laity recover the sense of their high calling as the people of God, and the shortage of clergy will not greatly matter.

We do not properly possess anything in the realm of the spirit until we have given it away.

When Jesus gave his disciples a pattern prayer his eyes scarcely strayed from this world to the next.

Let us stop to make quite sure we are not British men and women first and Christians afterwards.

The most fatal spiritual disease to which we can succumb is getting used to our Christian faith.

Surely God the perfect Creator is no admirer of slipshod work.

Rules can make us do better, but not our best.

Resolutions cannot change our nature; but they can help God to change us.

Sometimes repentance is pride masquerading under another name - a feeling that we have let ourselves down.

We can always think up good reasons for doing what we have set our minds on.

God uses many means, of which calamity is one, to throw us into each other's arms.

Words are not necessary in thanksgiving; to understand and to act - these are the necessary things.

The world's judgment of Christ and the world's judgment of his disciples go on side by side.

A common delusion of British people is that reverence means being miserable rather than joyful.

The use of our gifts is the true way of happiness; it is how we give ourselves away.

Mary Magdalene mistook Jesus for the gardener; he told us to mistake the gardener for him.

The lectern, no less than the altar, is an appointed rendez-vous with God.

Let us for God's sake make ourselves uncomfortable.

Doubt is neither a sin nor a virtue, but a challenge.

We must at one and the same time own and disown our sin, that God may create a new future for us.

Death is the end of life, and the beginning of life which has no end.

If our faith were strong enough we should, like Jesus, turn out of the house of death those who weep and wail.

If we look at the Acts of the Apostles and still say, 'You can't change human nature', we are guilty of blasphemy.

If we believe that 'spiritual' is the opposite of 'material', we cannot hold the Christian faith.

We live by the word of God and the bread of God and the breath of God. Those were the gifts of Jesus to his disciples.

Doctrine must affect life, or there is no point in it.

Human love is not revealed by word of mouth or by proxy, but in person and in action; so is God's.

Printed in the United Kingdom
by Lightning Source UK Ltd.
108262UKS00003B/46-63

9 781905 565054